I0722074

FIELD TRIPS

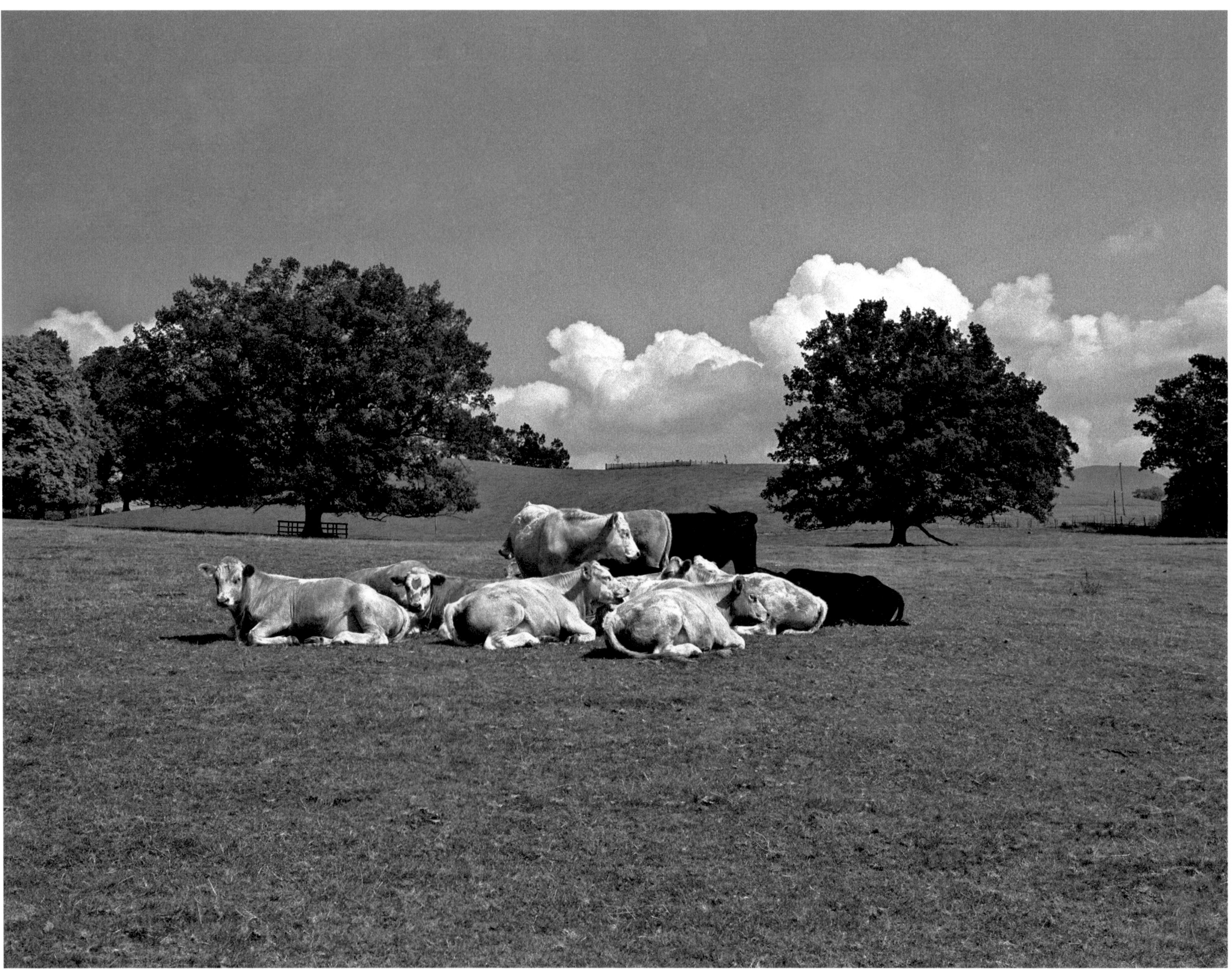

FIELD TRIPS

TRAVELS IN BRITAIN 1976-1993

Berris Conolly

DEWI LEWIS PUBLISHING

OUT OF TIME, OUT OF PLACE

Travis Elborough

I normally tell people I grew up beside the sea. But it's perhaps more accurate to say I grew up beside the A27.

The relentless tides of traffic on this road – which straddles the length of the south coast from Hampshire to East Sussex – were as much a constant feature of my Worthing childhood as the waves on the local beach.

My father had worked for a time in the motor trade in Hove, his daily commute along this road taking him past the twin towers of the old coal-fired Shoreham B Power Station at Southwick – a monolithic brick building long since lost that was Sussex's answer to Battersea's Pink Floyd sleeve-gracing plant, and the tallest structure for miles around.

While its chimneys no longer belched filthy smoke, the plant having closed a year or two earlier, I imagine that the emissions from my father's Ford Cortina were hardly less toxic for the environment. I certainly don't remember unleaded being an option on the pumps of the fairyland-sounding Elf garage he usually visited en route.

But such asphalt roads, along with concrete underpasses and motorways, the zenith of petrol-powered traffic, loomed far larger back then: *Two-Lane Blacktop* and the possibilities of endless motion, part Beat writer revelry and part Ballardian nightmare with a bit of *Genevieve* thrown in for good measure. (The London to Brighton Veteran Car Run ended locally after all.)

The A27 would also convey me and my primary school classmates to Arundel Castle, in the kind of chrome-grille fronted and tartan interior filled British Leyland motor coach that seemed the transport of choice for teams of blazer and tie wearing footballers on Cup Final days.

This was on the very first field trip that I can remember. Though I think it was perhaps more likely referred to as 'an outing' or even 'a day out', its duration confirmed by the fact that midway through, sandwiches of slimy fish paste on white sliced bread and sealed in cling film, and orange squash in polystyrene cups were doled out. No concessions here to any dietary requirements, the squash a shade of orange not seen so often in the wake of the rolling back of tartrazine.

Arundel Castle is just 9 miles along the A27, and had proximity and history on its side. Though as I was to discover in more recent years, little of the original medieval castle remained even then and the bulk of it is, rather like Tower Bridge, something of a Victorian steampunk sham, with even its impressive collection of suits of armour bulk-bought in the closing decades of the nineteenth century when the high Gothic and all things Arthurian held sway.

But to a gaggle of seven or eight year-old kids who'd had *The Hobbit* read to them in class and were mad on *Star Wars*, it seemed as magical as Gandalf or The Jedi Knights, and was probably a lot more fun for being largely stage-set fake.

I recall that a trip the following year to Bramber and its ruined castle, singularly failed to match up to it. The castle, rubble by any other name really, had only a decidedly underwhelming gatehouse (or what was left of it) and some grass ditches to show for itself.

Its authenticity and eerie beauty counted for little at that age, perhaps much in the way that back then a banana-flavoured Nesquik drink was infinitely preferable to a dull old banana, what with its peel and all those stringy bits that you had to pull off before you could eat the damned thing.

Fortunately this trip was saved by a bonus stop at an additional Bramber attraction: a museum whose highly specialised collection it strikes me was probably of rather limited, if not outright dubious, pedagogical value at this stage in our education.

The House of Pipes, as its name suggests, was an institution given over entirely to said smoking implements, its spongy white plastered walls lined, and glass cabinets stuffed, with examples that ranged from simple clay models to the hubble-bubble hookah ilk favoured by the caterpillar in *Alice's Adventures in Wonderland*.

The museum's proprietor had the girth and hirsuteness of the wrestler and World of Sport mainstay Giant Haystacks. But he had a gentle manner and spoke in a high, squeaking register that rendered him comic rather than sinister, and while conducting the tour exchanged a few knowing confidences about the qualities of certain pipes with our form teacher Mrs Sergeant. Exchanges that suggested she was better acquainted with hookahs than we might previously have realised.

Though given that she sported floor-length burlap skirts, a surplus of beaded jewellery, and long, lank centre-parted hair and rarely passed up an opportunity to whip out her acoustic guitar in lessons, the signs were probably there.

She'd also helped organise this visit to the museum, so must have possessed at least a passing acquaintance with pipes, or at least, felt that we children might need to know something about them to grow into fully formed adults in the coming Age of Aquarius.

Otherwise why were we there? The whole justification for field trips was that we should learn something from them.

My parents to a degree subscribed to this way of thinking too when it came to days out and holidays, where a certain purposefulness prevailed.

The beach and the South Downs were on our doorstep, and therefore always the easiest options for many happy days spent lazing on the former or walking about the latter. But if we were to go somewhere else then it must be to see or do something, preferably a site of supposed natural beauty, a stately home, a National Trust garden, a cathedral, a monument, a zoo or wildlife park, a museum, aquarium, or a preserved railway.

And all reached by car and providing me with a backseat view of B-road Britain into the bargain.

Art galleries never featured in my parents' itineraries. Like abroad, they were somewhere I wouldn't venture to until my late teens and with a far more cultured, and better-travelled, art school girlfriend. Though we might see pictures, watercolours or oils of the almost painting by numbers variety (or 'along' with TV's Nancy Kominsky) at innumerable (or more accurately, interminable) craft markets and fêtes that my mother, a trained seamstress/curtain maker, liked to frequent out of semi-professional interest.

However, steam fairs, with traction engines billowing plumes of off-white smoke and tottering about the place as unsteady as many of the attendant pensioners on their feet, and country shows with parades of vast bullocks and much pinning of rosettes on prize pigs, with not a growth hormone or factory farming pen in sight, seemed ubiquitous.

That industry and agriculture, or romanticised and largely bankrupt versions of them, had by the late 1970s and early 80s already become firmly established branches of tourism and, for us, a leisure activity or a form of entertainment, was perhaps more telling than I could have realised about this nation's subsequent direction of travel.

In about 1981 or thereabouts, I was given, or possibly inherited, a camera from some family member or other. It was an aged Kodak Brownie 127 of questionable vintage whose curved black Bakelite body and cream plastic shutter button and winder knob made it look like an art-deco radio set, though it hailed from the 1950s or early 60s.

The most basic of point and shoot cameras and sturdy enough to suffer whatever my 10/11 year-old hands could throw at it, this Brownie, despite its obvious datedness when Space Invaders and Disc Cameras were all the rage, became one of my most prized possessions. For the next couple of years it accompanied me on whatever excursions we subsequently made.

For reasons of parsimony and the fear that I'd just waste the then seemingly more expensive colour film, my parents would only buy me black and white stock.

I was also under strict instructions to take as few photographs as possible. Which given that you only got 8 frames per roll rather limited my photographic output to about one snap per excursion.

But I still have the first photograph I ever took. A dinky square job with white borders, that preserves the monochrome impression of hulking great Highland cattle, these beasts with horns that could helmet about two dozen Vikings. This picture, just about in focus and actually not bad for a first attempt, was taken at Killerton Park in Devon during one of the many summers we spent in the West Country, as often as not staying with my grandparents.

After running a pirate themed eatery in Polperro in Cornwall called The Jolly Roger, they had by this time moved to Lyme Regis and established a B&B along no less nautical lines: the breakfast menus were leatherette-bound and decorated with golden compass points and written in an indecipherable copperplate script that made ordering a Full English feel like a hunt for buried treasure.

But my memories of this period are forever, I was going to say, coloured but, of course, the reverse is true, de-coloured arguably, by the few precious black and white pictures I have of those vacations and outings. And as poorly shot and out of focus as many of them were, it is how I see those times in retrospect and it is, in turn, partially what I find so arresting about Berris Conolly's photographs.

For here, if you like, are documents from a yesterday that I remember so well but had almost begun to doubt ever existed at all. It's proof perhaps that there is nothing so distant and strange as the recent past. These are places out of time and a time now long out of place. Haunts could easily be an alternative title, for there is often something genuinely ghostly about the lost world they show, with even a washing line in Norfolk appearing to be possessed by wraiths and a graveyard of tyres at Hampole outside Doncaster that could very nearly be skulls.

The time frame of these pictures runs from 1976, with its famously hot summer of water shortages and infestation of ladybirds soundtracked by Kiki Dee and Elton John's 'Don't Go Breaking My Heart' right up to 1993 and the height of rave, the doldrums of John Major's Conservative government and the horror of Noel's House Party and Mr Blobby. In between is a nation, and one largely depicted obliquely here, turned upside down by Thatcherism and deindustrialisation, council house sales, consumerism and containerisation. Though the latter is glimpsed in the image of Tilbury from 1985, twinned with a photograph of Port Talbot steel works from three years later, with what looks like Inspector Morse's vintage Jag parked up outside. And indeed the cars which stud many scenes here are often the clearest indicator of what era we are in. The boot of a Ford Escort Mark III at the edge of a frame, for instance, carbon dating us to the days when sat nav was still largely the stuff of science fiction.

People appear only fleetingly in Conolly's vistas and usually in the middle to far distance. One exception is his image of the front at Great Yarmouth which foregrounds three older ladies sitting on a bench, their heads wrapped in plastic hoods to keep the inevitable rain at bay. Behind them, however, is the incongruous alien presence of a life-size drawing of Darth Vader underscoring that while the sea itself might be sublime, Britain's beach resorts are frequently, and delightfully, ridiculous. Static caravans, fences, rusting signs for Lyons Maid ice cream – these are the true sights of the seaside these pictures remind us of again. And just round the corner from the

Royal Crescent, Bath's beauty lies in a telephone junction box.

Broken wood gates (marked 'Private'), and topiary alike in the late twentieth century countryside landscapes of Conolly uphold the invidious work of the enclosures acts of two hundred years earlier. The stones at Avebury similarly come braided with concrete posts and barbed wire, and this ancient monument complemented by a passing butchers' van, ley hunting by British Leyland, if you will. (Though I think the vehicle in question is actually a Bedford…)

Nevertheless, there is a touch of Alfred Watkins's own photographs from *The Old Straight Track* about the images of the byways of Wales and Devon.

Yet Conolly has a penchant for the symmetry of curving paths, culs de sac and streets that loop round on themselves or peter out with the suggestion of dead ends; more literally in the case of the A625, a tarmac-rucked roadway across the Peak District at Mam Tor fatally curtailed by constant landslips.

But elsewhere surreal directional signs and road markings seem to direct us to nowhere or nowhere in particular. A path to a playground in Arkwright Town in Derbyshire appears to give up the ghost before reaching its destination. Somewhat prophetically as it turns out, since all of the children Conolly snapped gaily playing on the swings in this former Coal Board mining town would later be moved out and the whole place levelled due to methane leakage.

Contrary to L P Hartley, the past, as Geoff Dyer has rightly observed, is not a different country at all, it is very much this country: Britain and there's no getting away from it. But here is a place of landlines, phone boxes and overhead pylons rather than wind farms, 5G masts and QR codes. The physical analogue present had yet to be subsumed by the digital, distant and virtual.

A bulky video camera wielded by what looks like a tourist, if notably kept at a safe distance from the Royal Albert Docks by a stretch of the Mersey and a hefty iron chain, is about as high tech as things get. If again possibly another harbinger of our current times where no landmark is free from the attention of phone-wielding visitors.

The footage from Conolly's field trips, on the other hand, is all about the legwork and has the mileage to show for it too.

A day out, three or four decades on, takes us to another time and another place entirely, something we call history. What we choose to learn from it is anybody's guess, but like the late House of Pipes it's well worth making the journey.

Travis Elborough, 2025

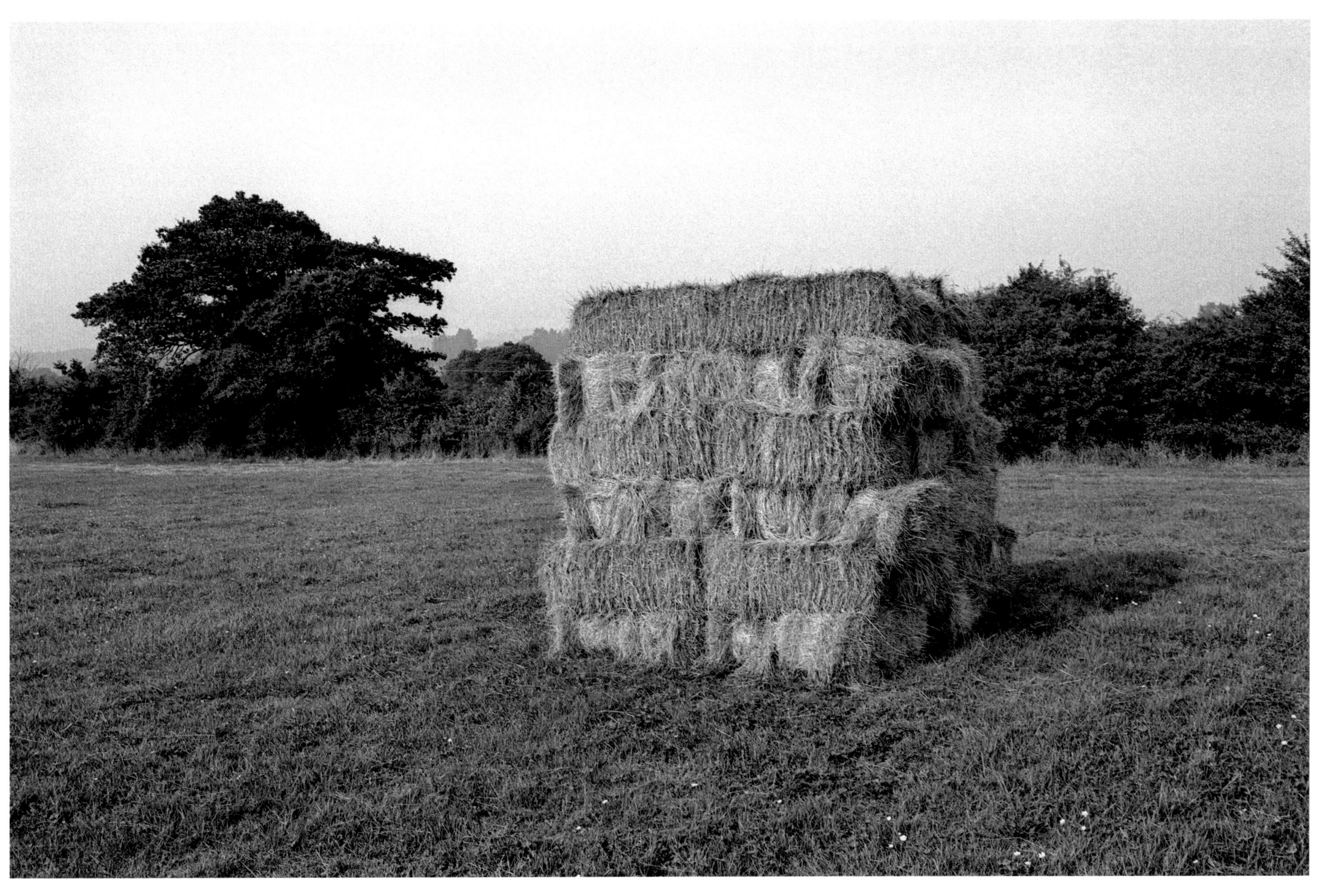

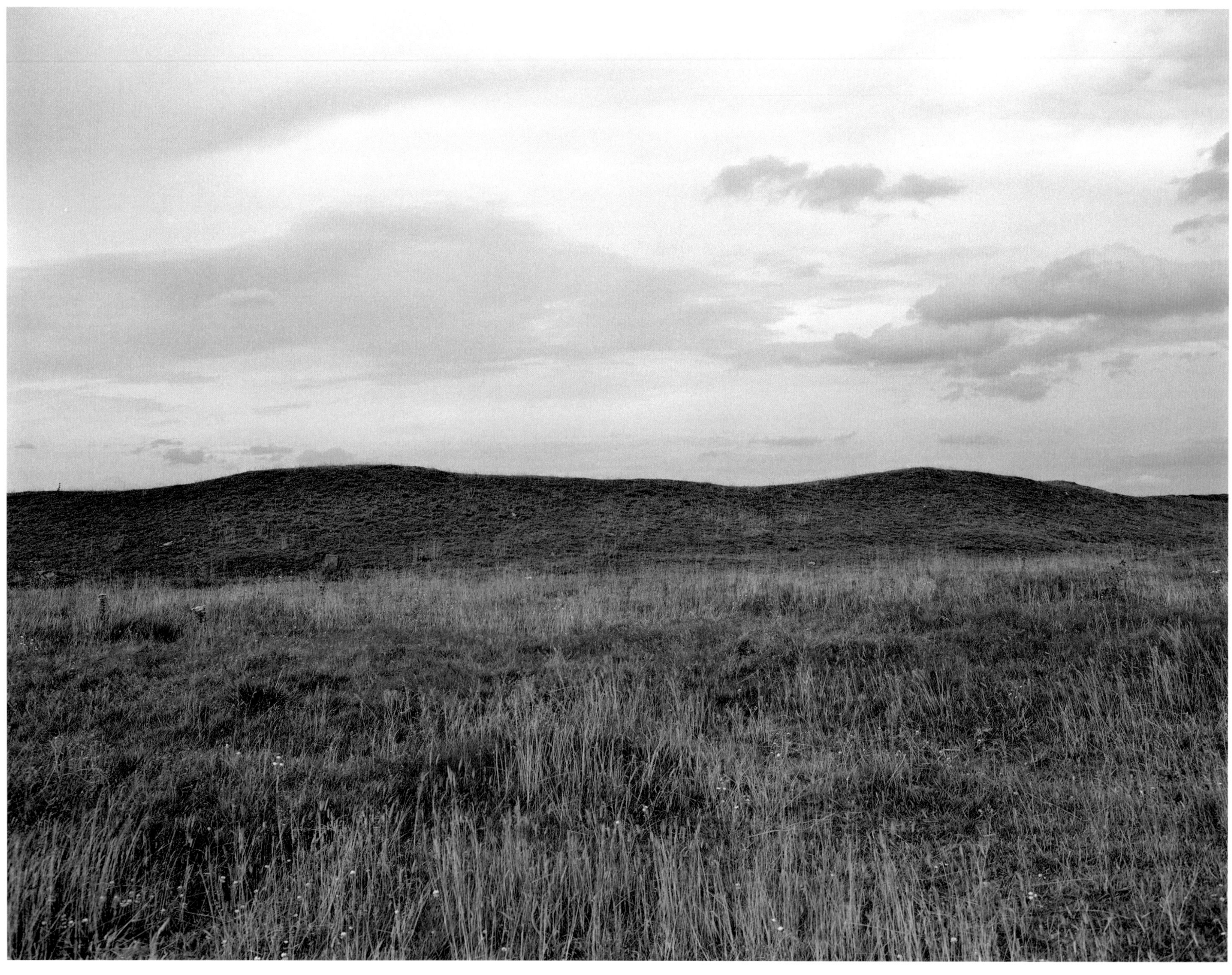

     Arbor Low, 1986

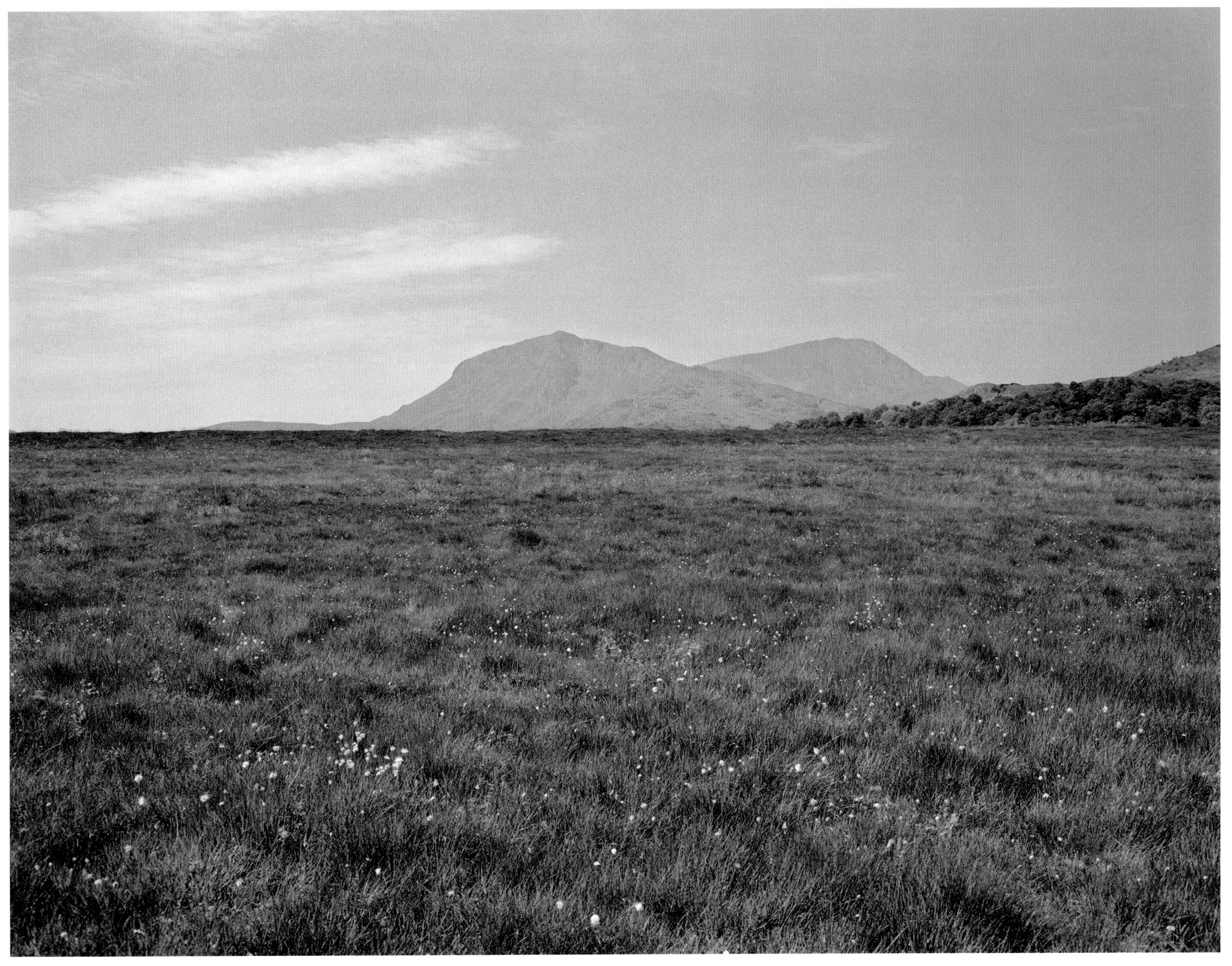

Cader Idris, 1987

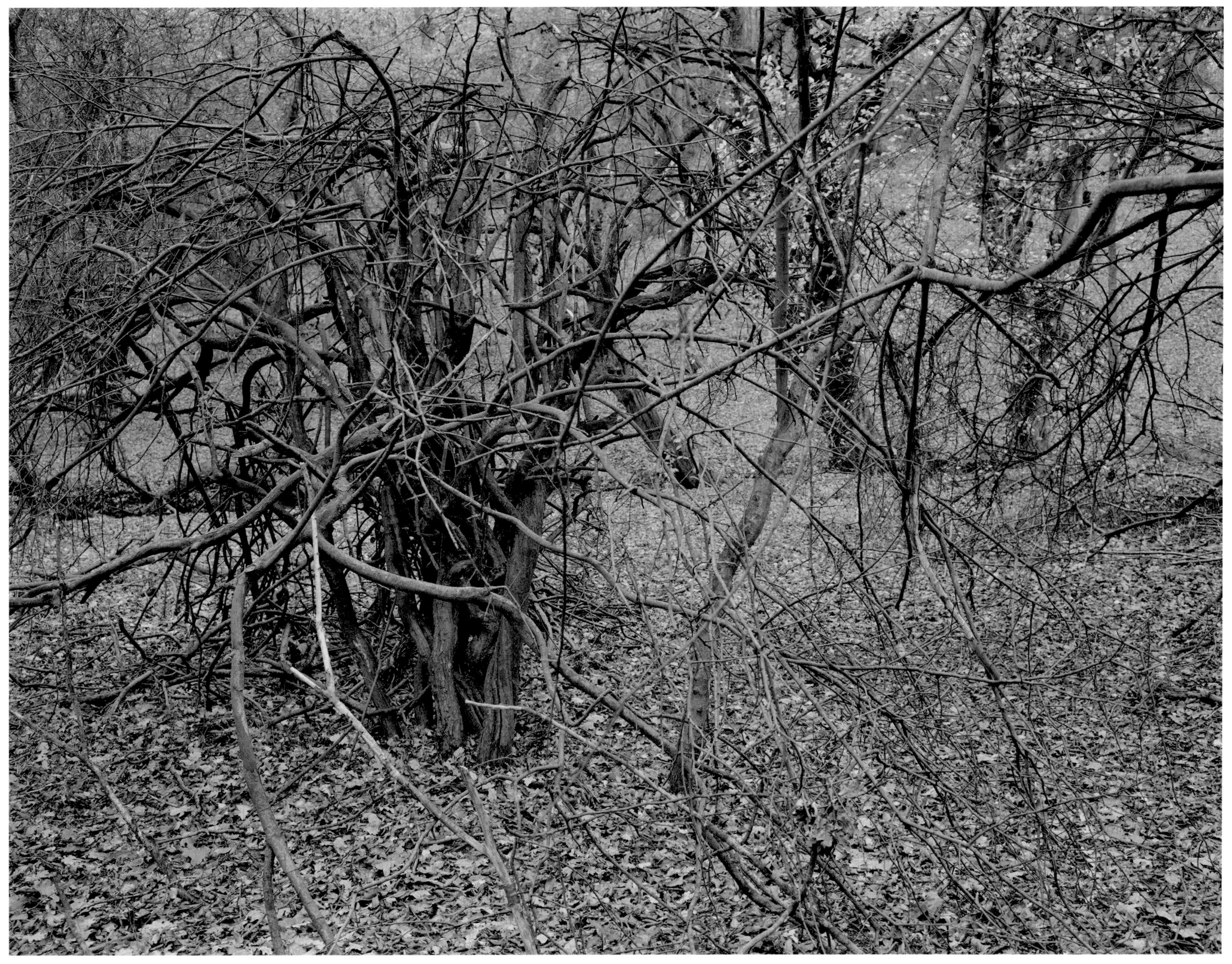

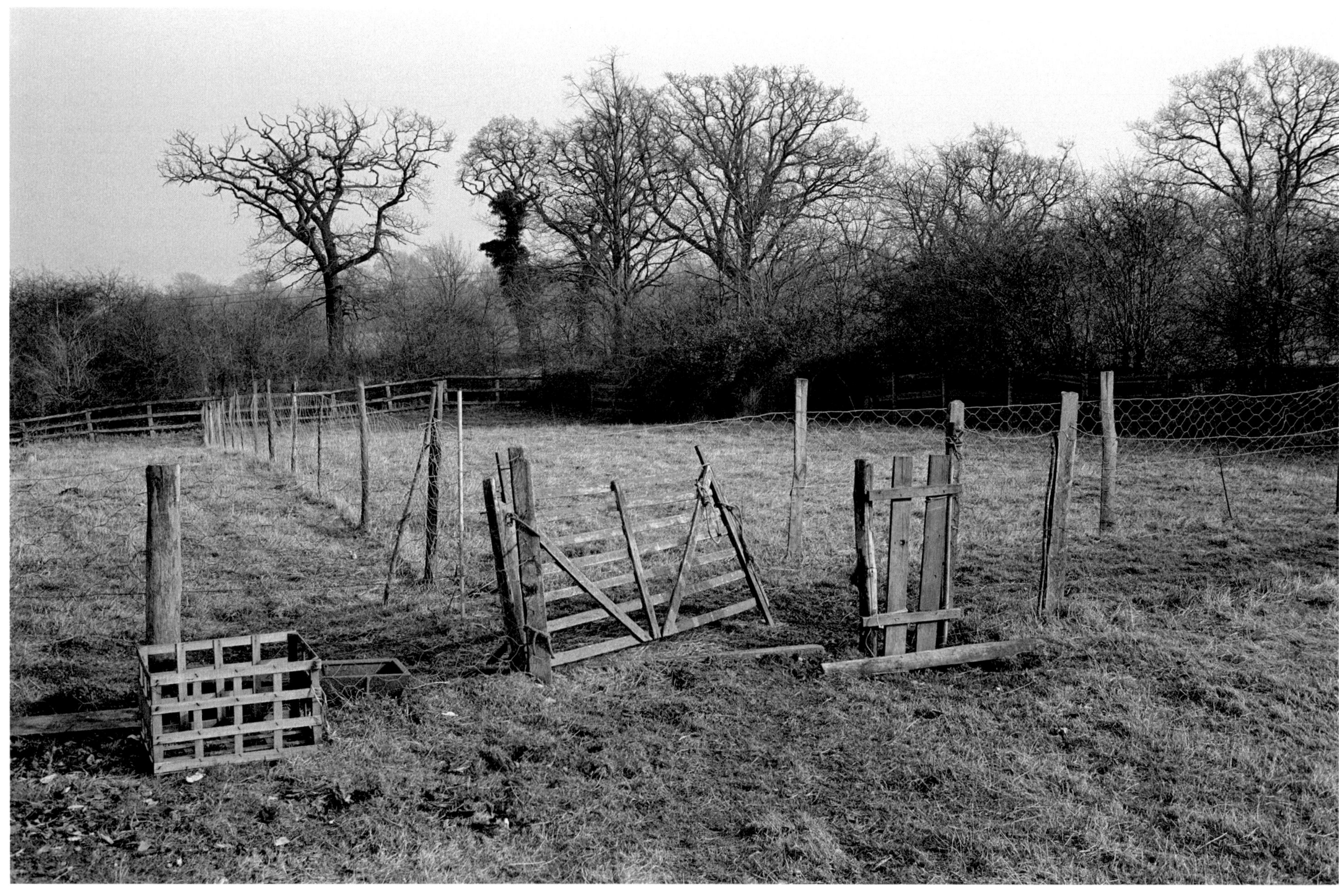

Essex, 1983

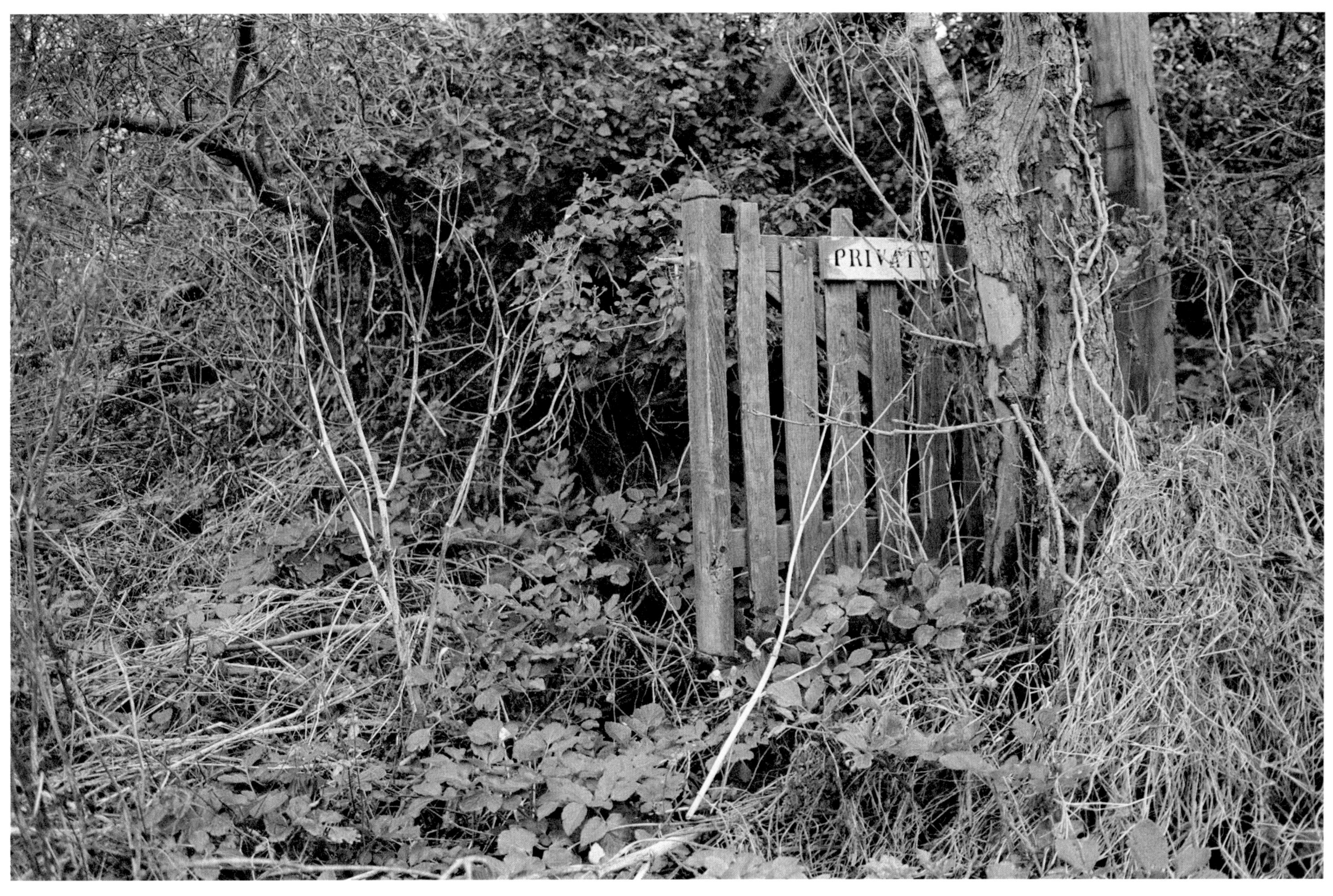

Suffolk, 1988

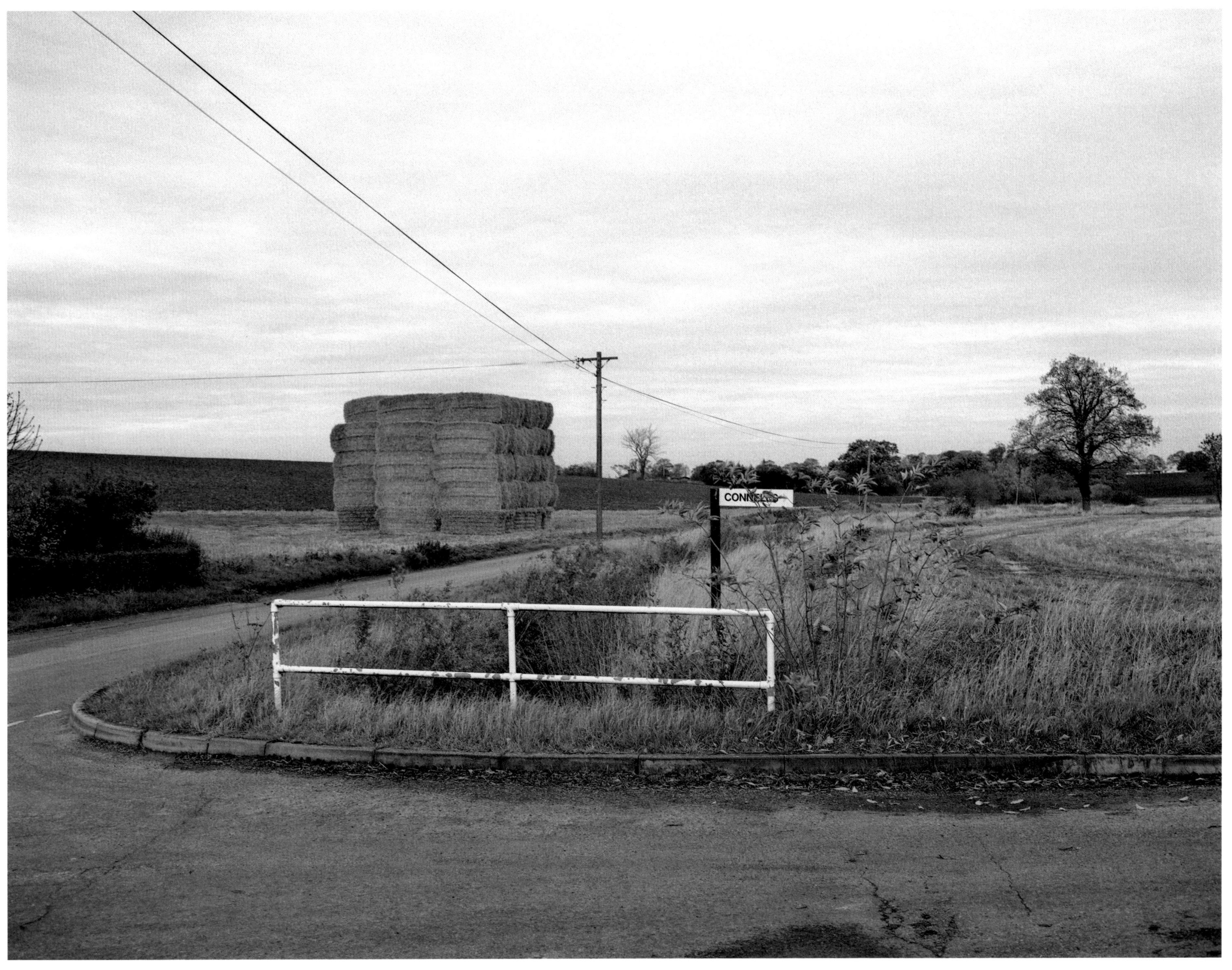

Suffolk, 1987   19

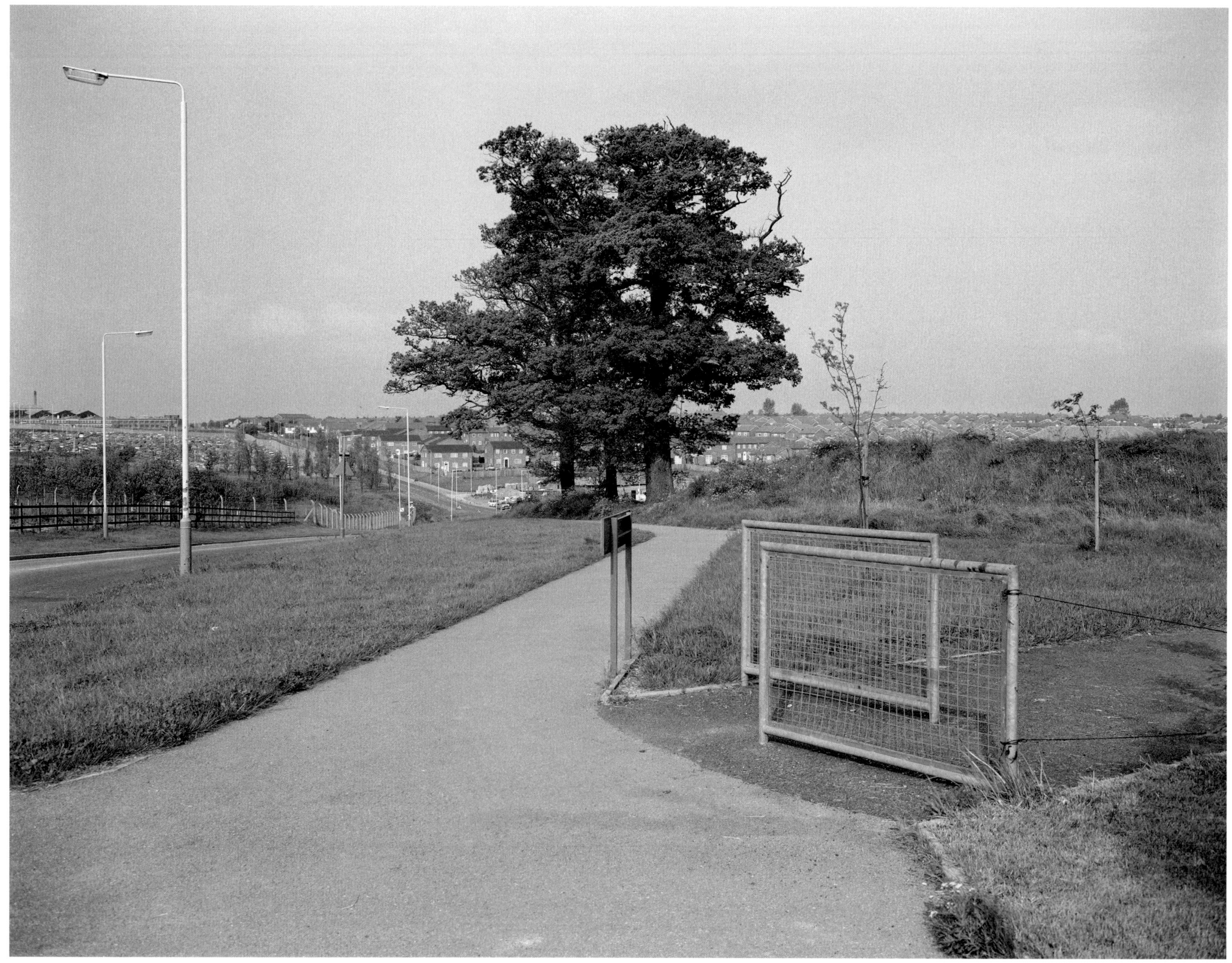

          Luton, 1988

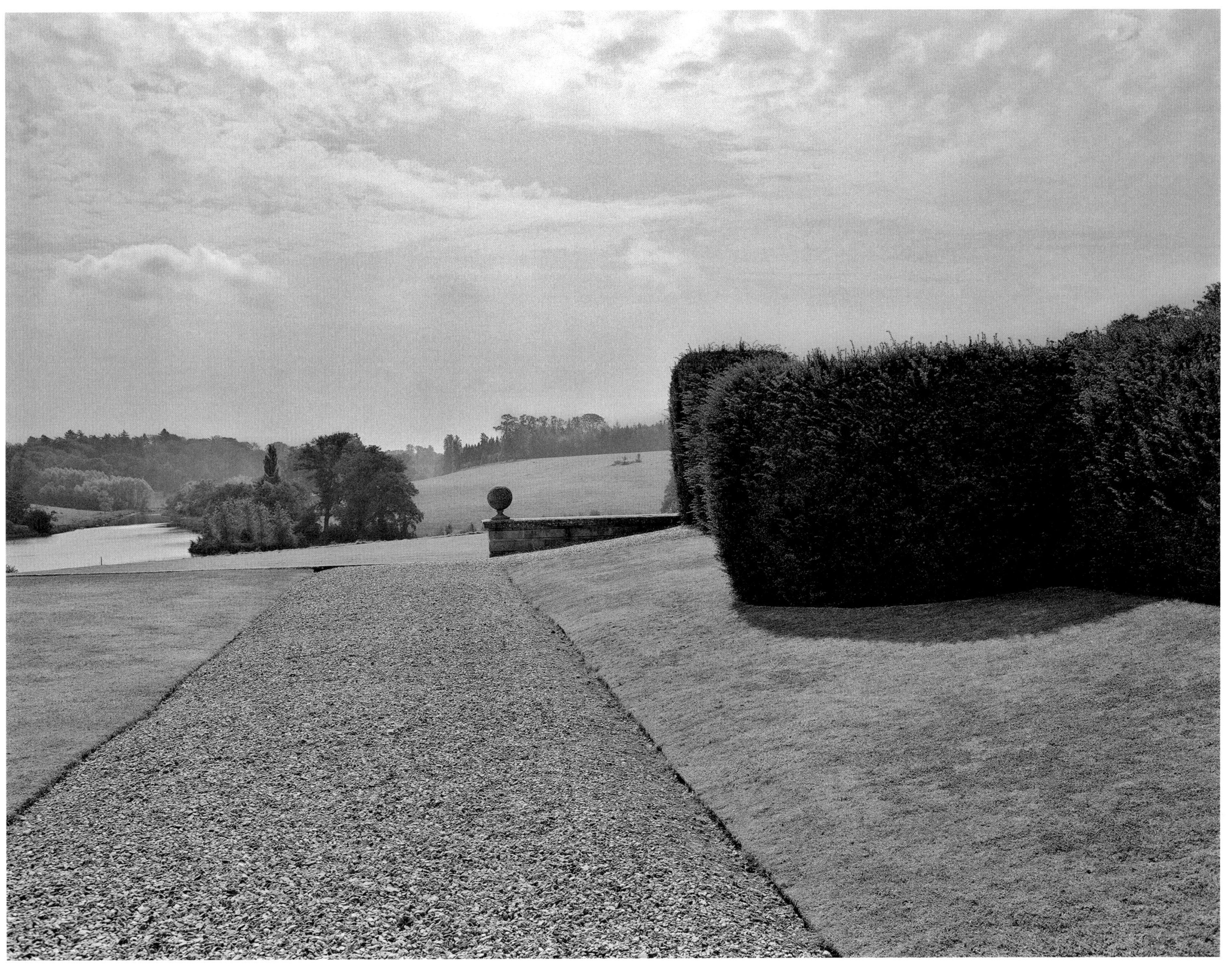

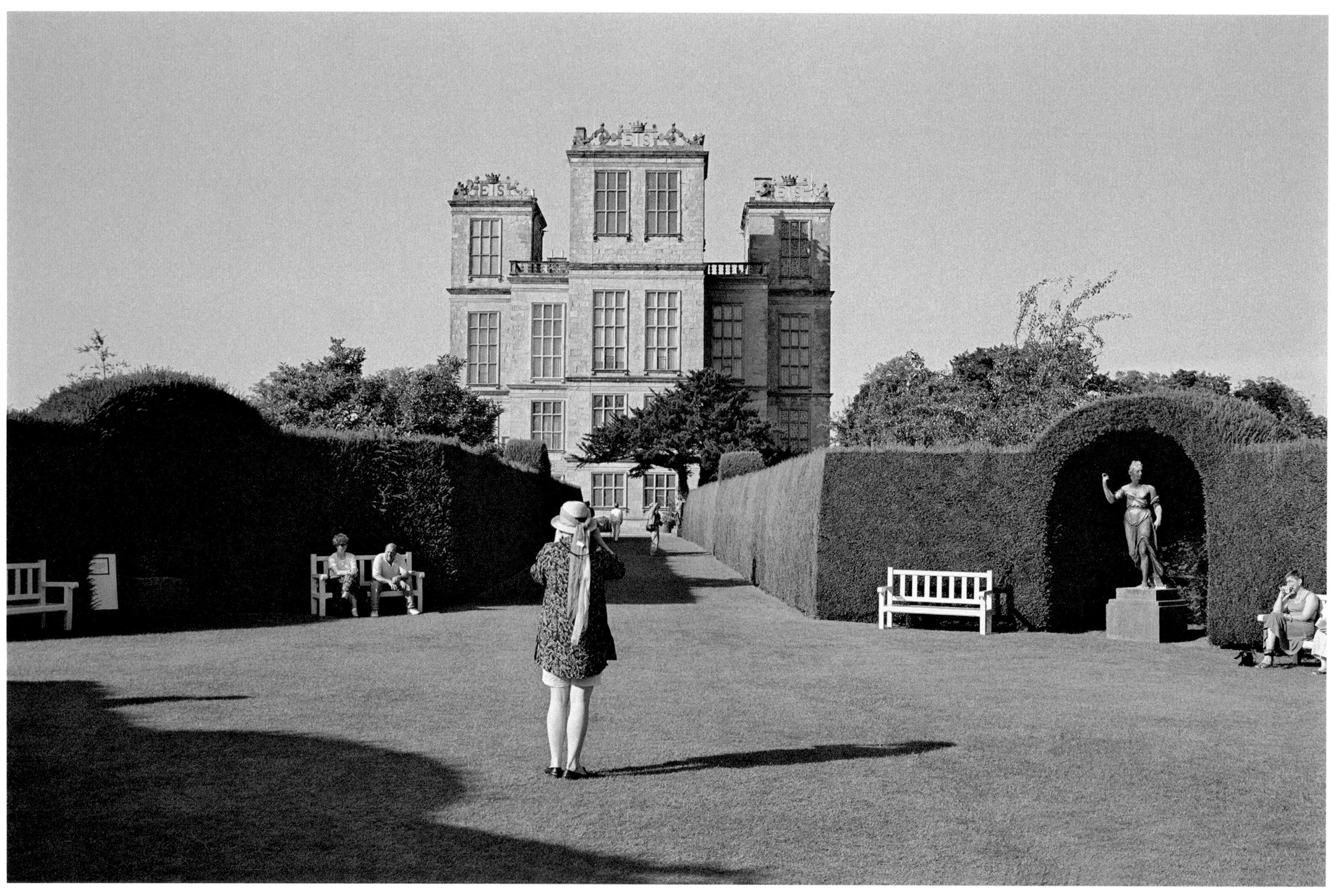

22   Hardwick Hall, 1991

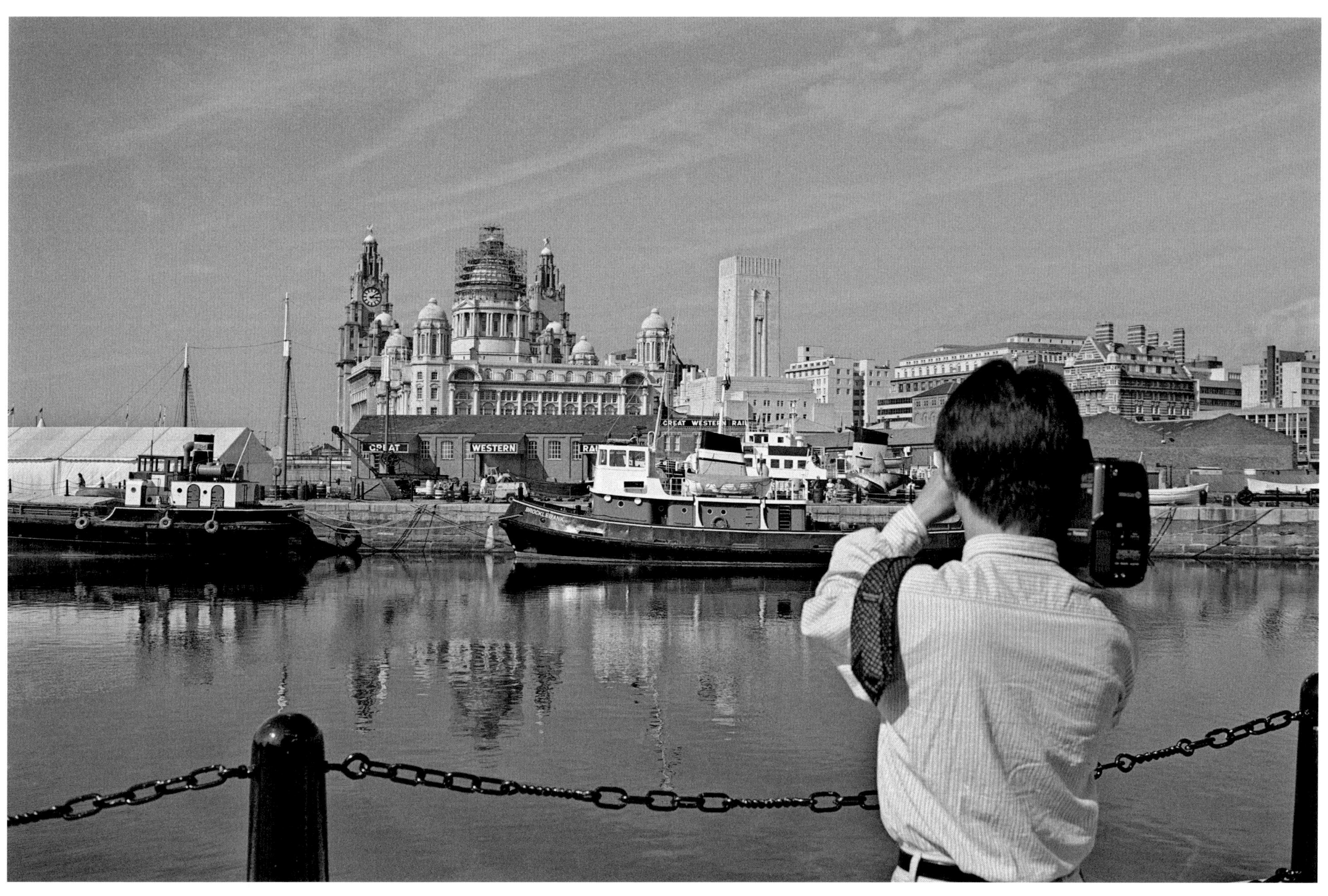

Liverpool, 1991

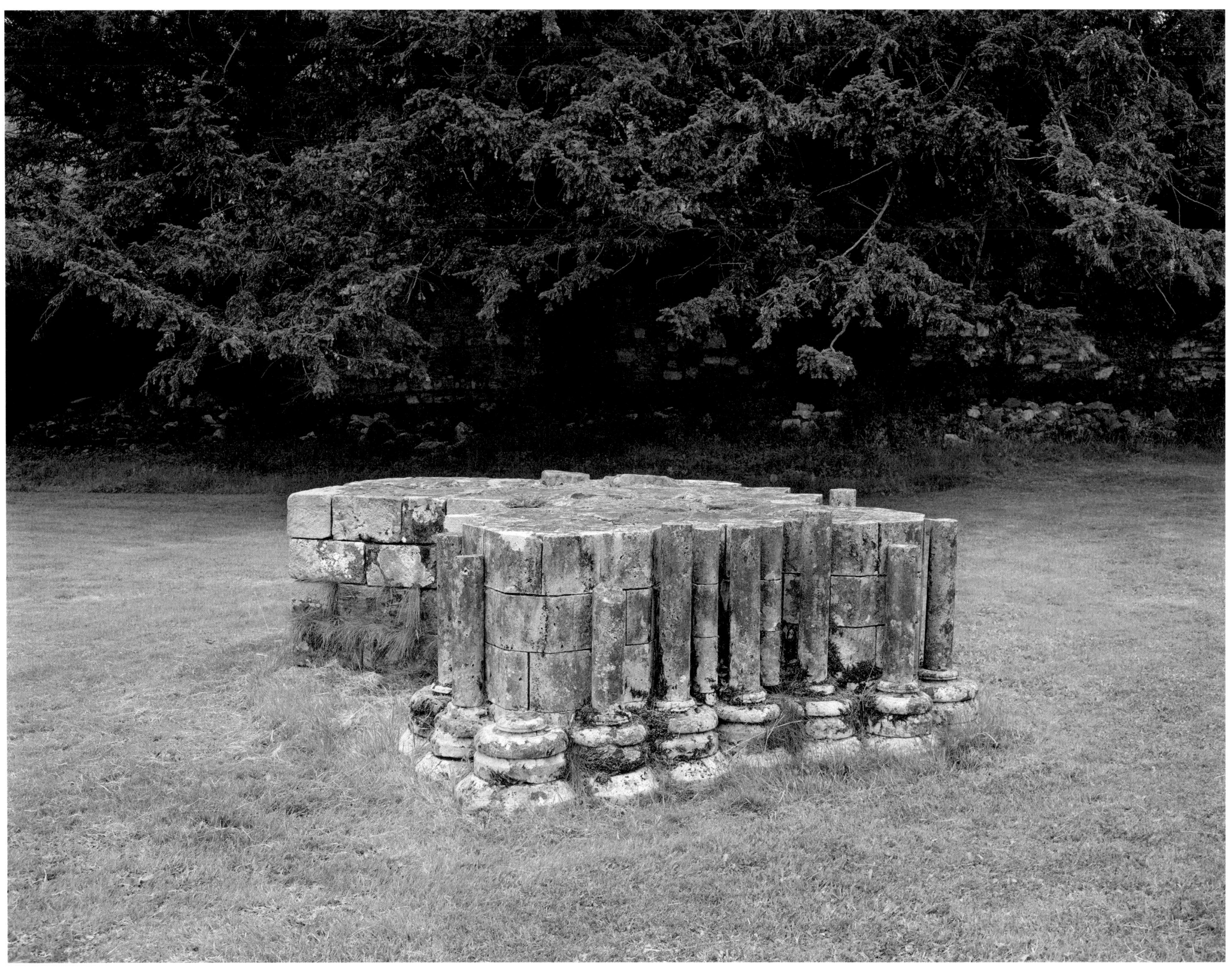

		Margam Abbey, 1988

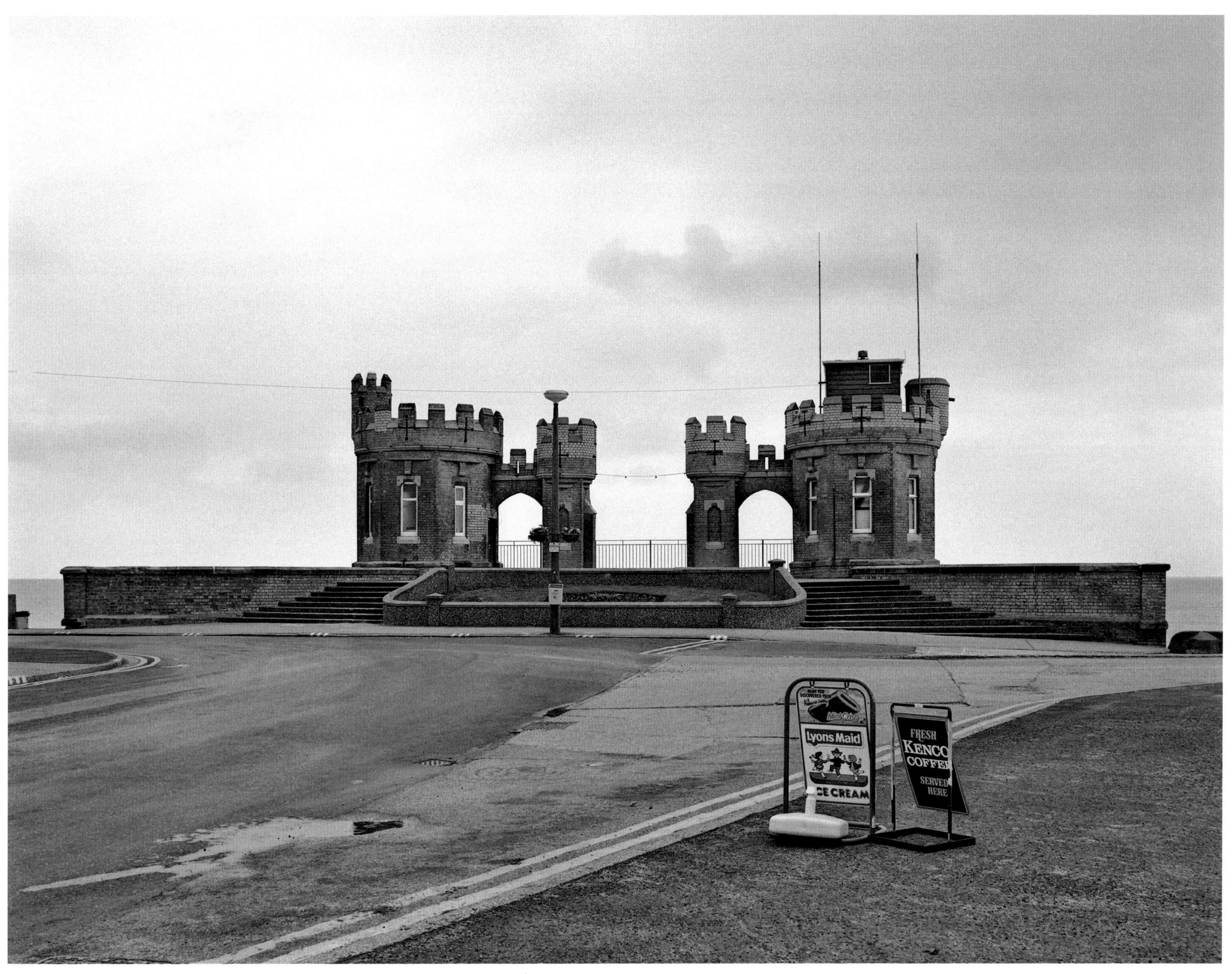

Withernsea, 1990

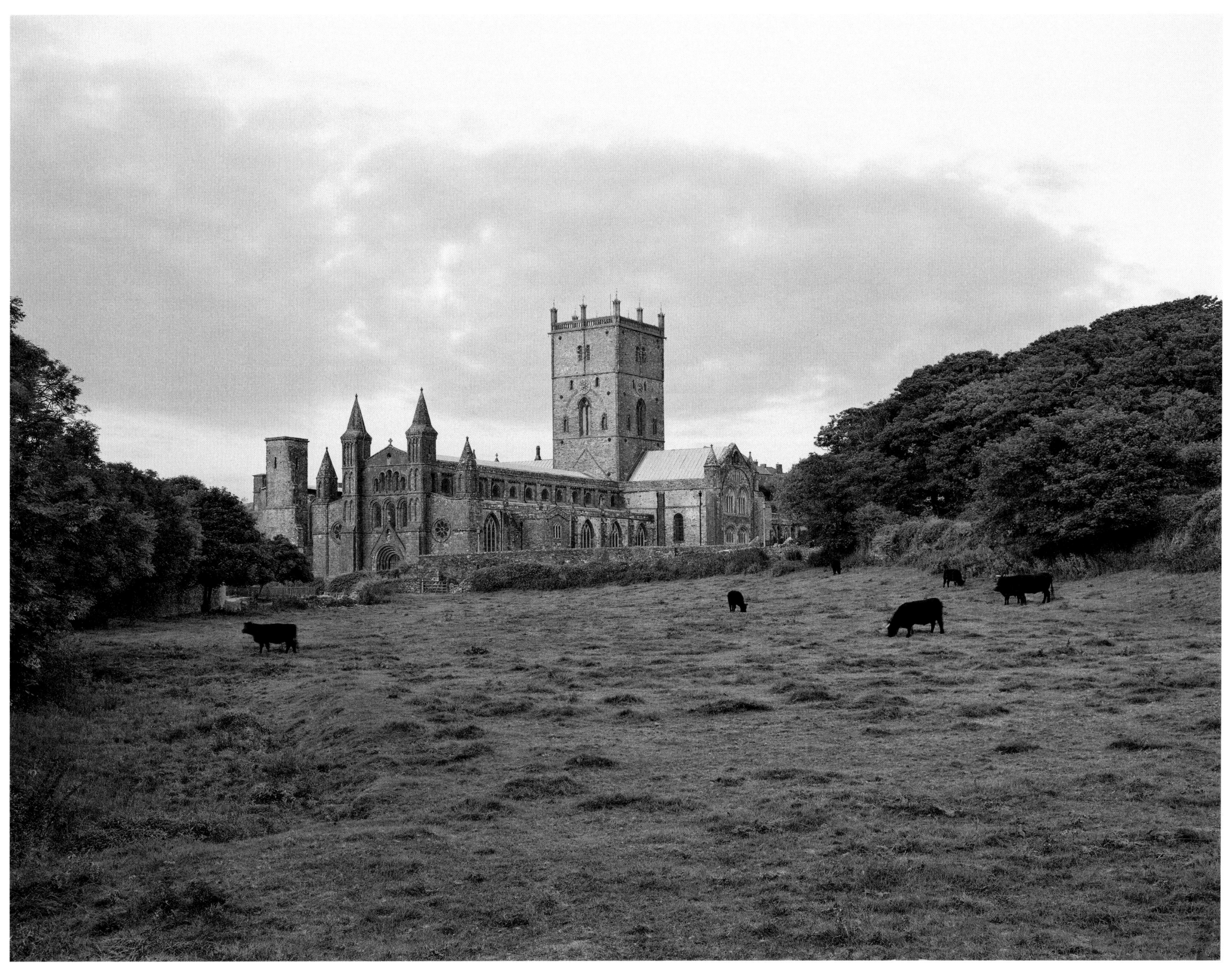

St David's, 1987

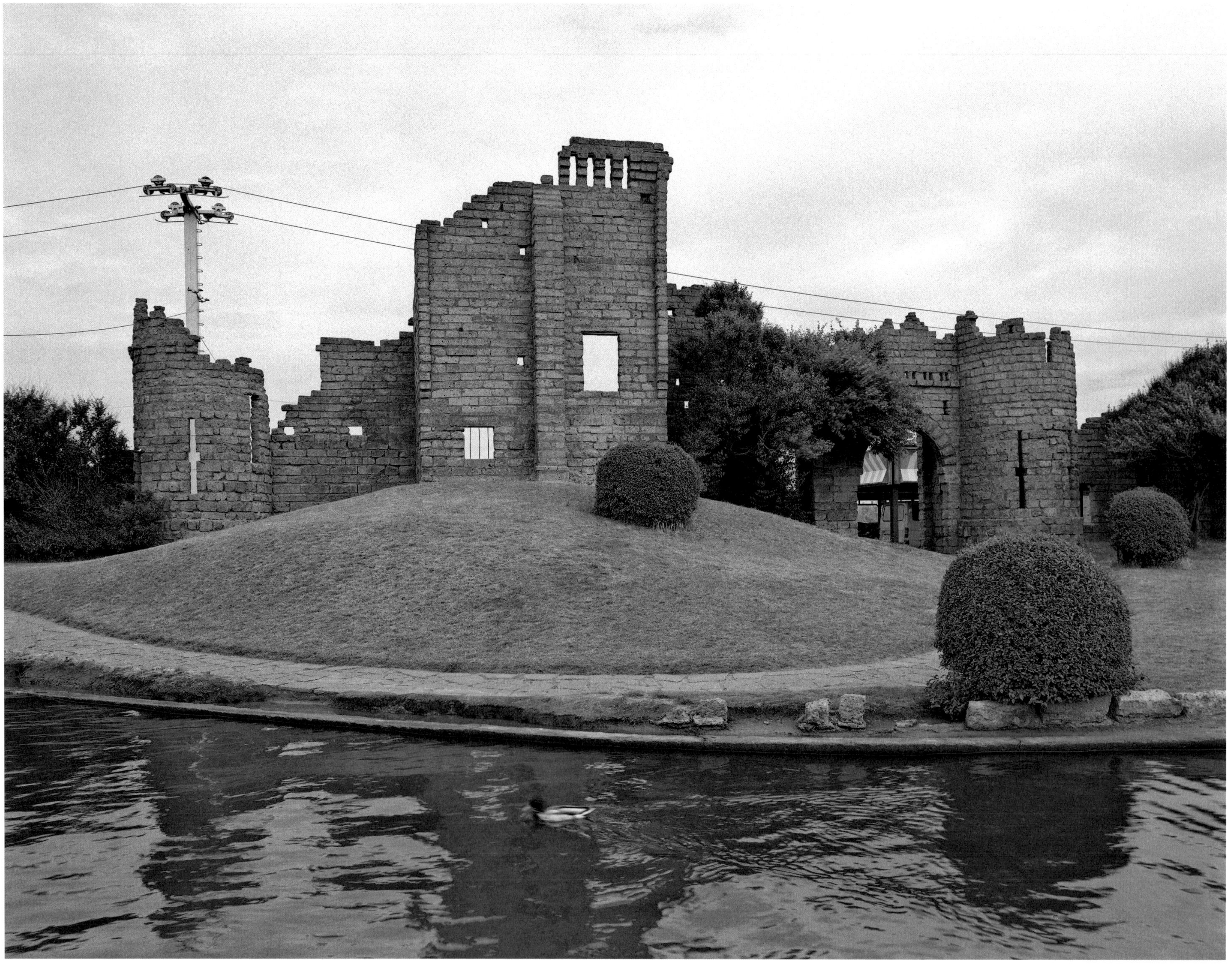

Skegness, 1990

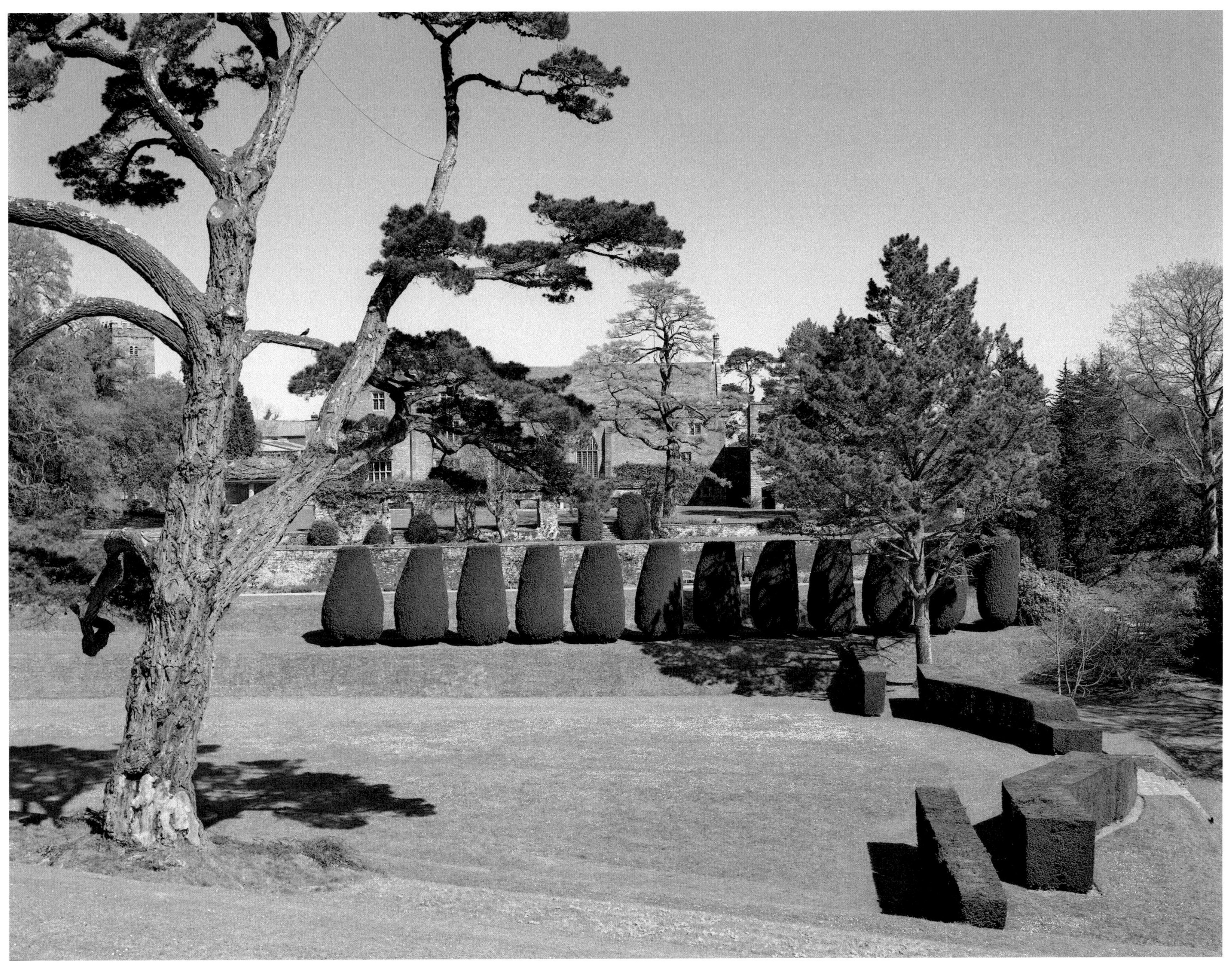

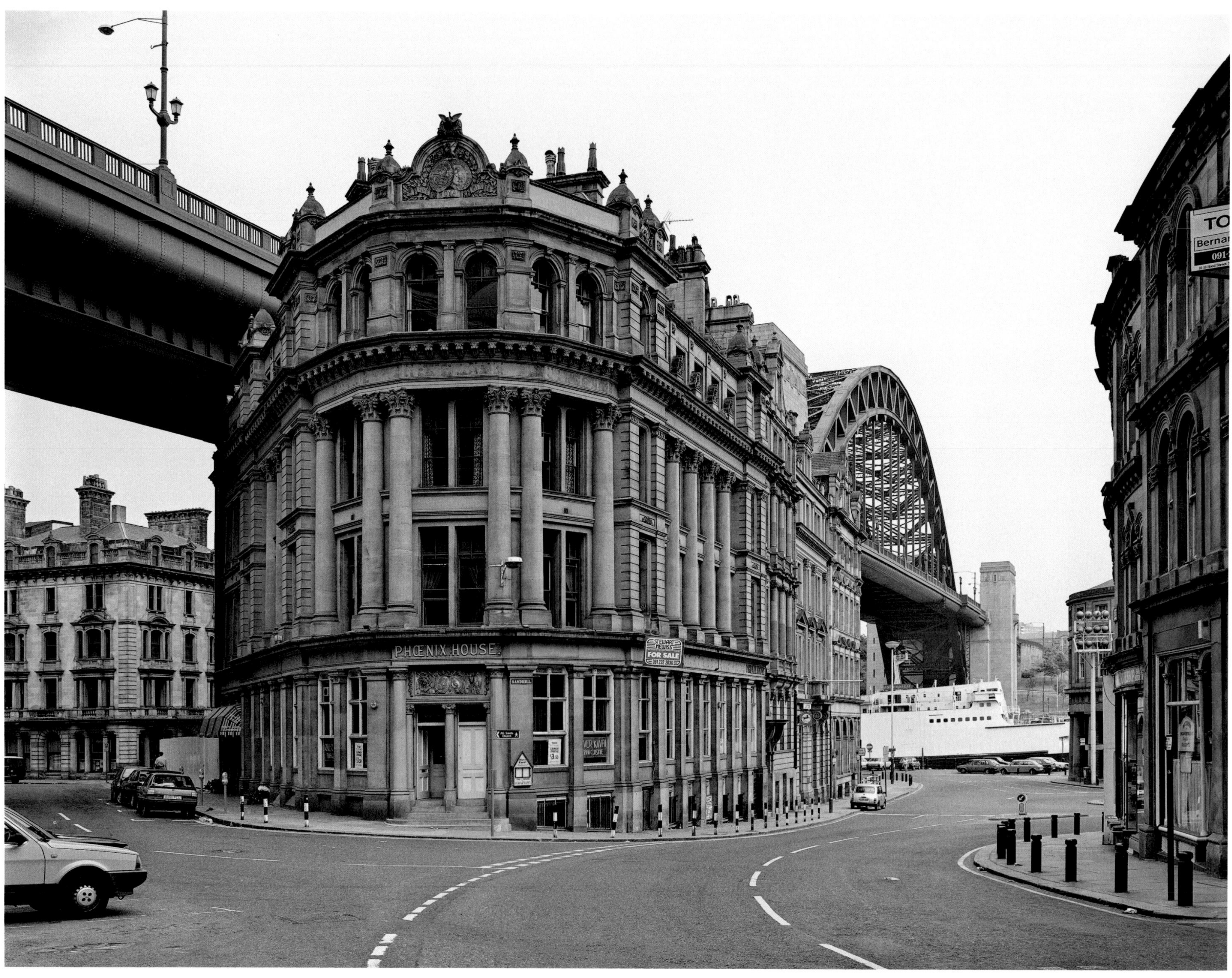

     Newcastle, 1989

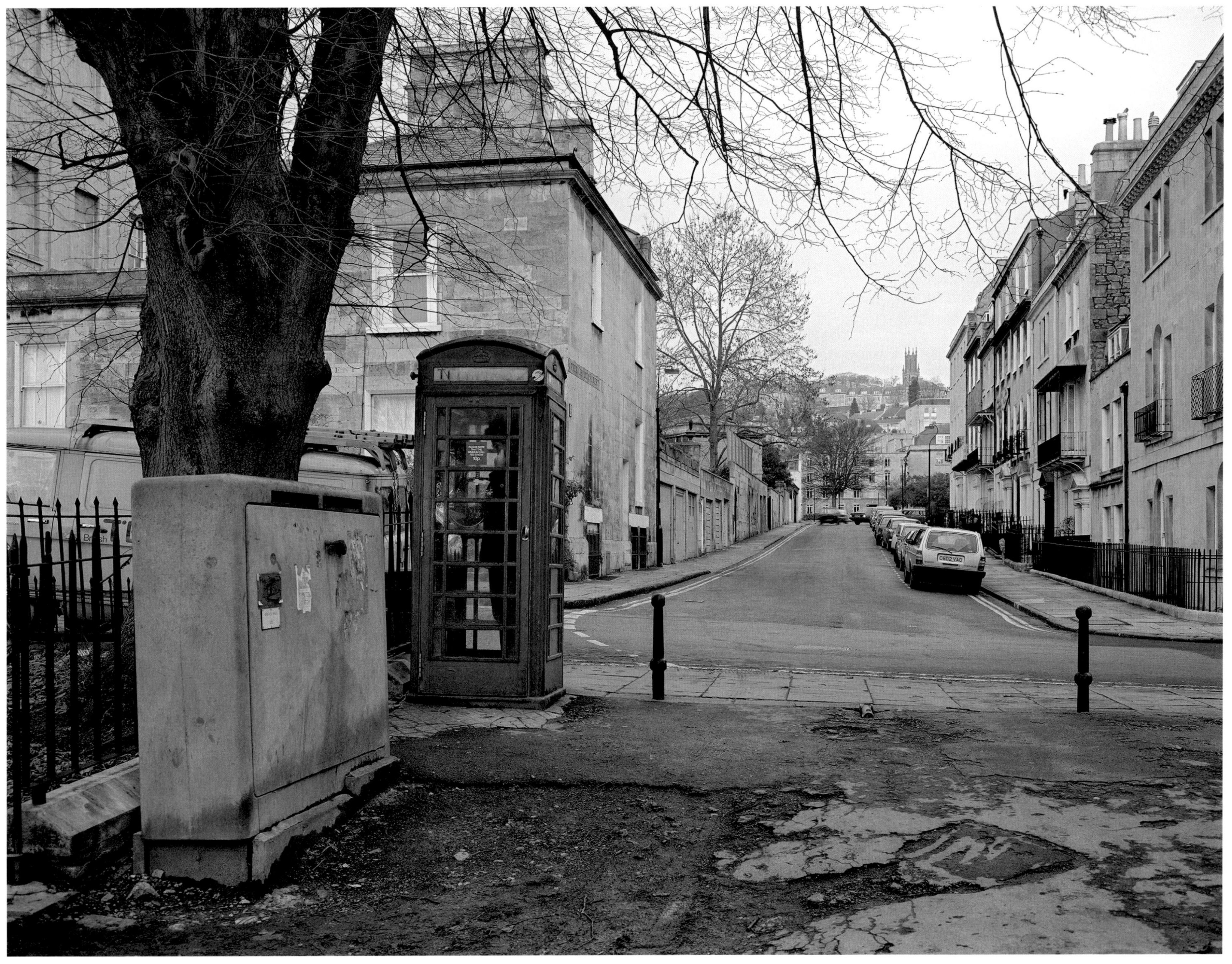

Bath, 1985

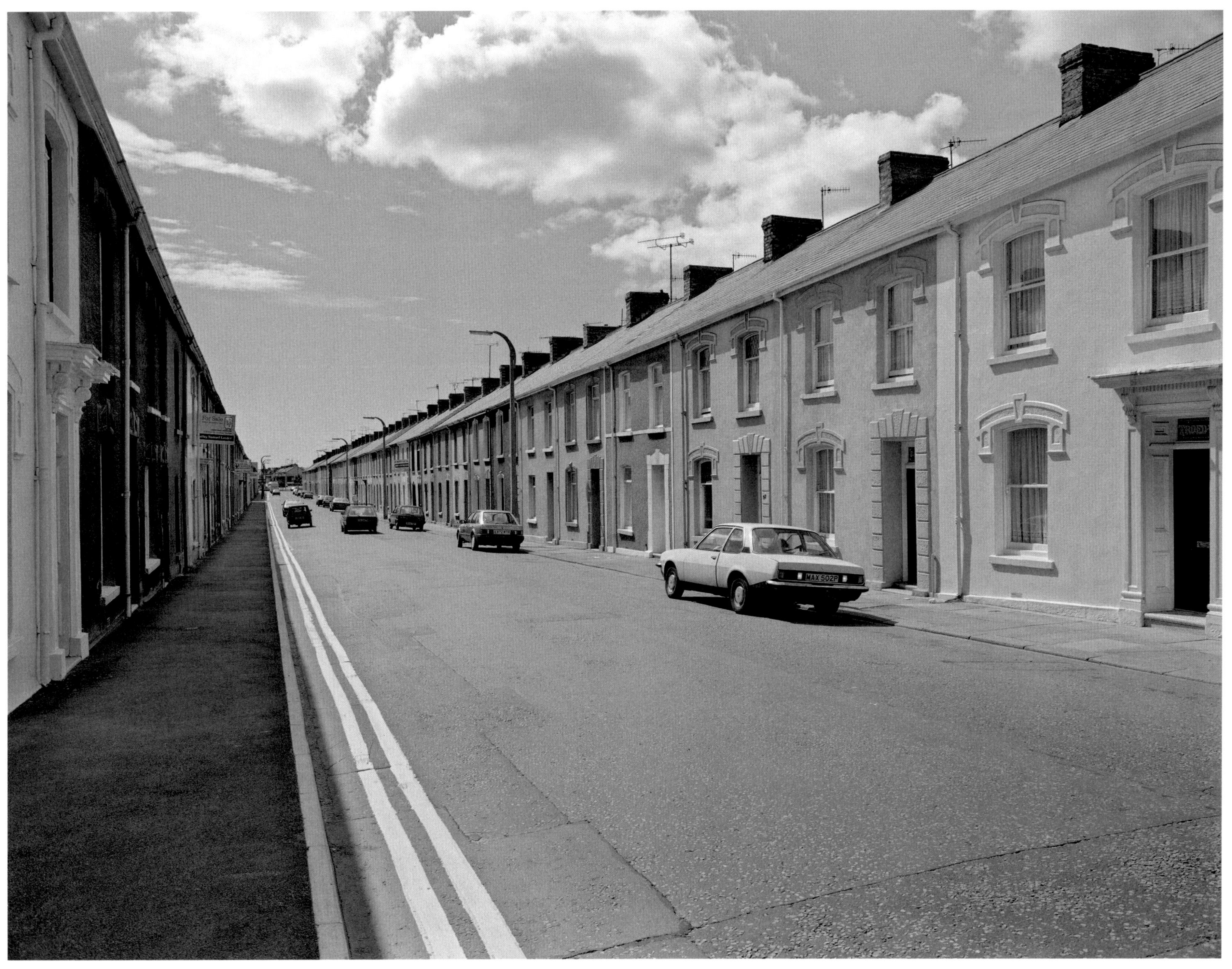

Llanelli, 1988

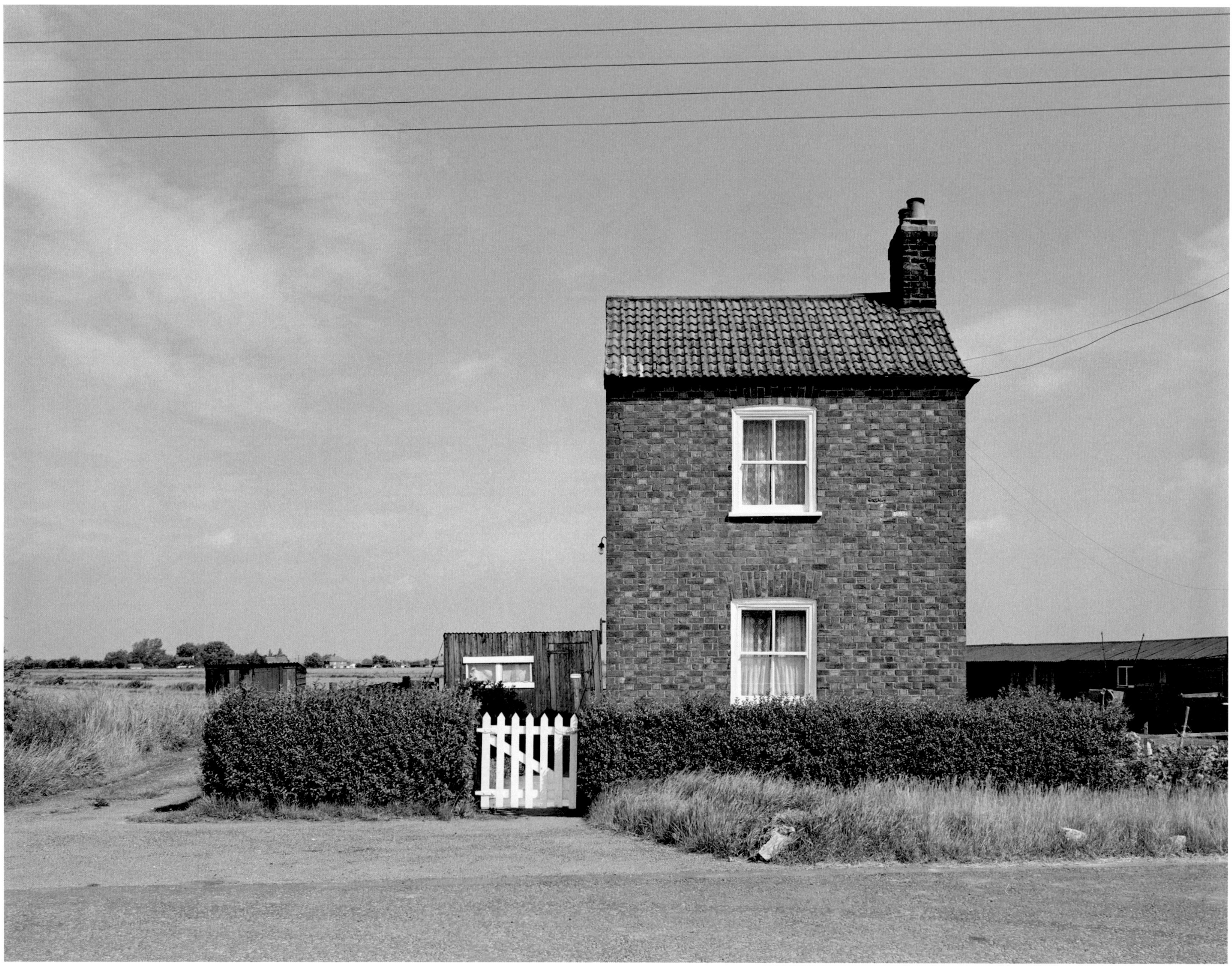

34   Lincolnshire, 1990

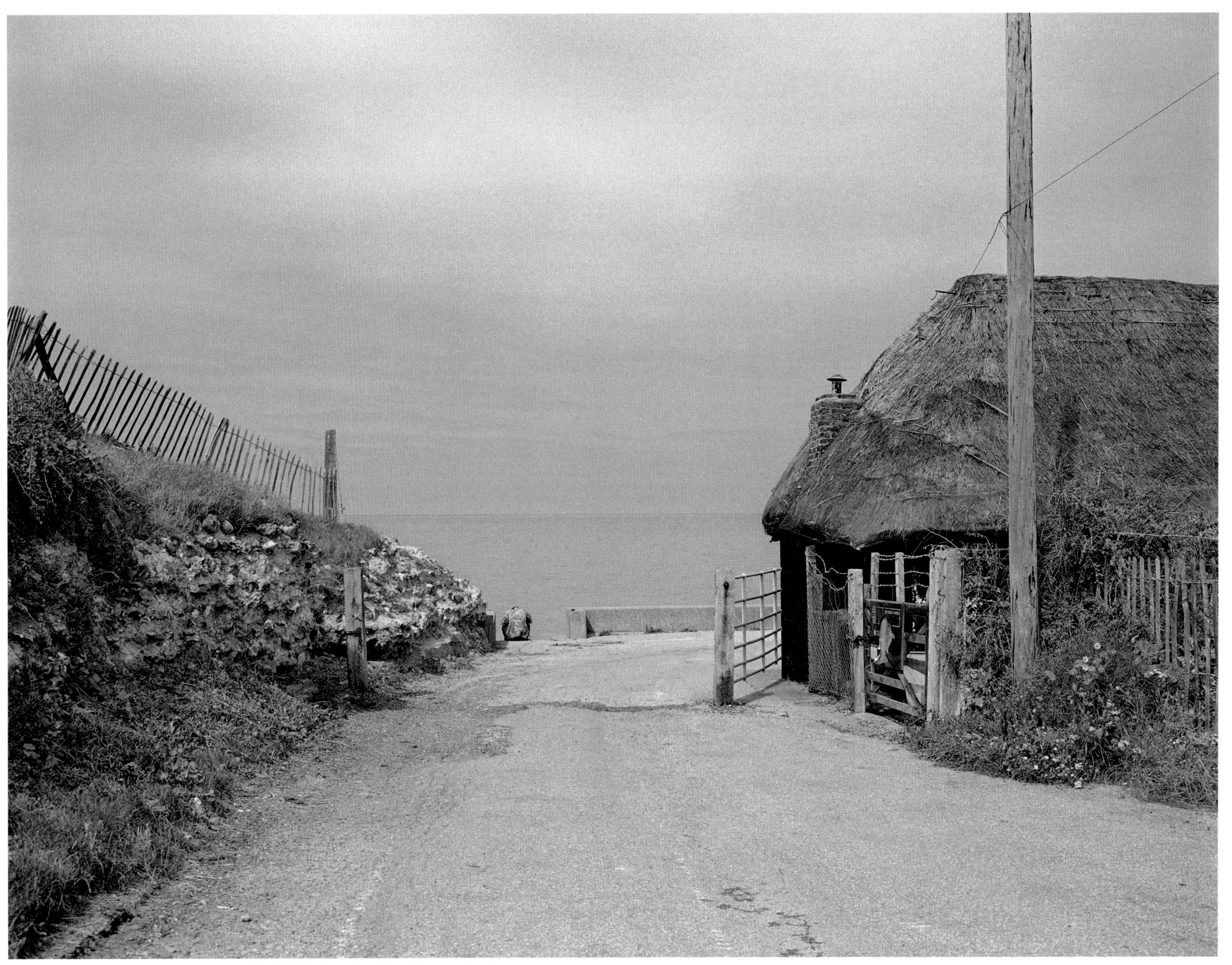

Roman wall, Reculver, 1987

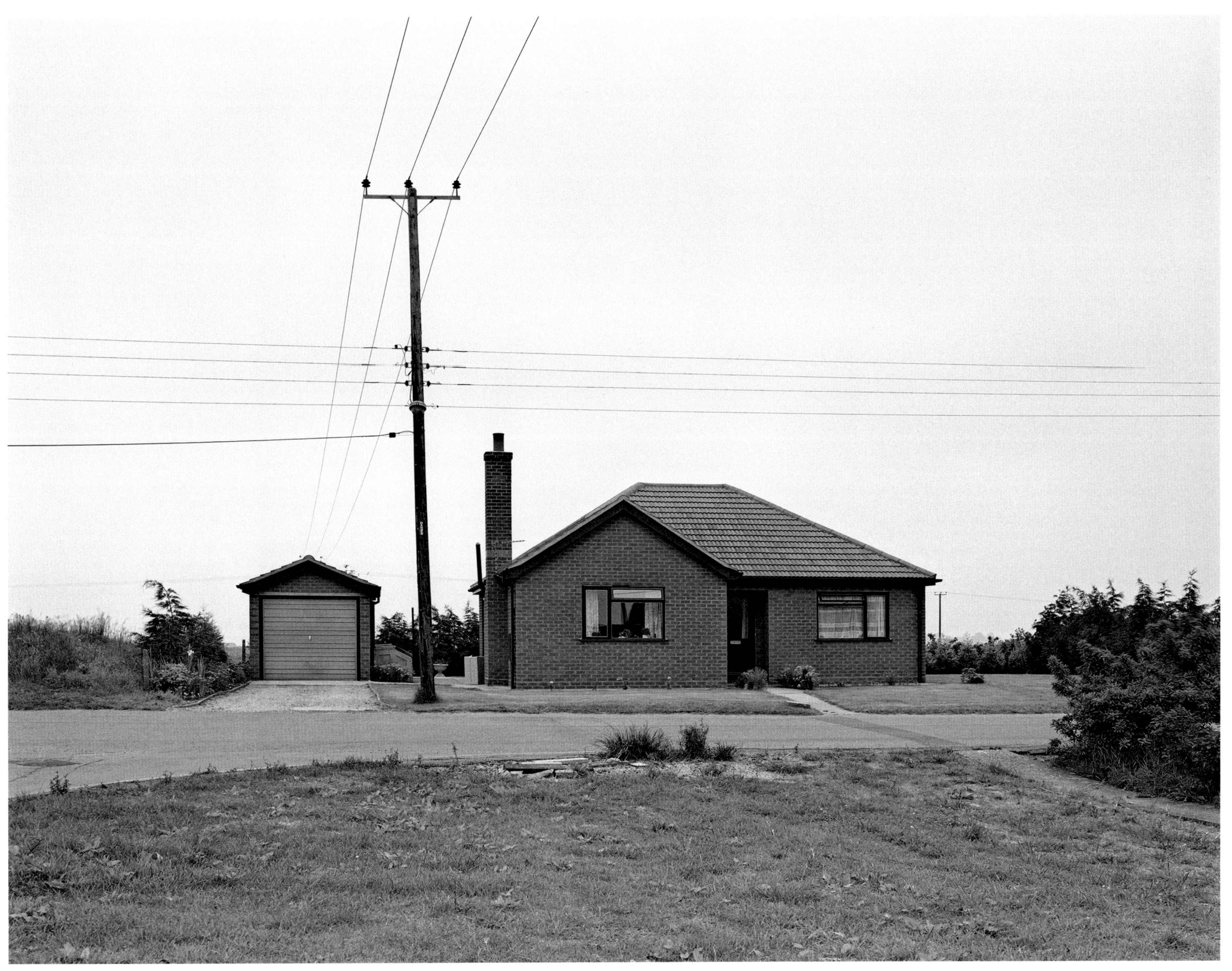

Lincolnshire, 1990   37

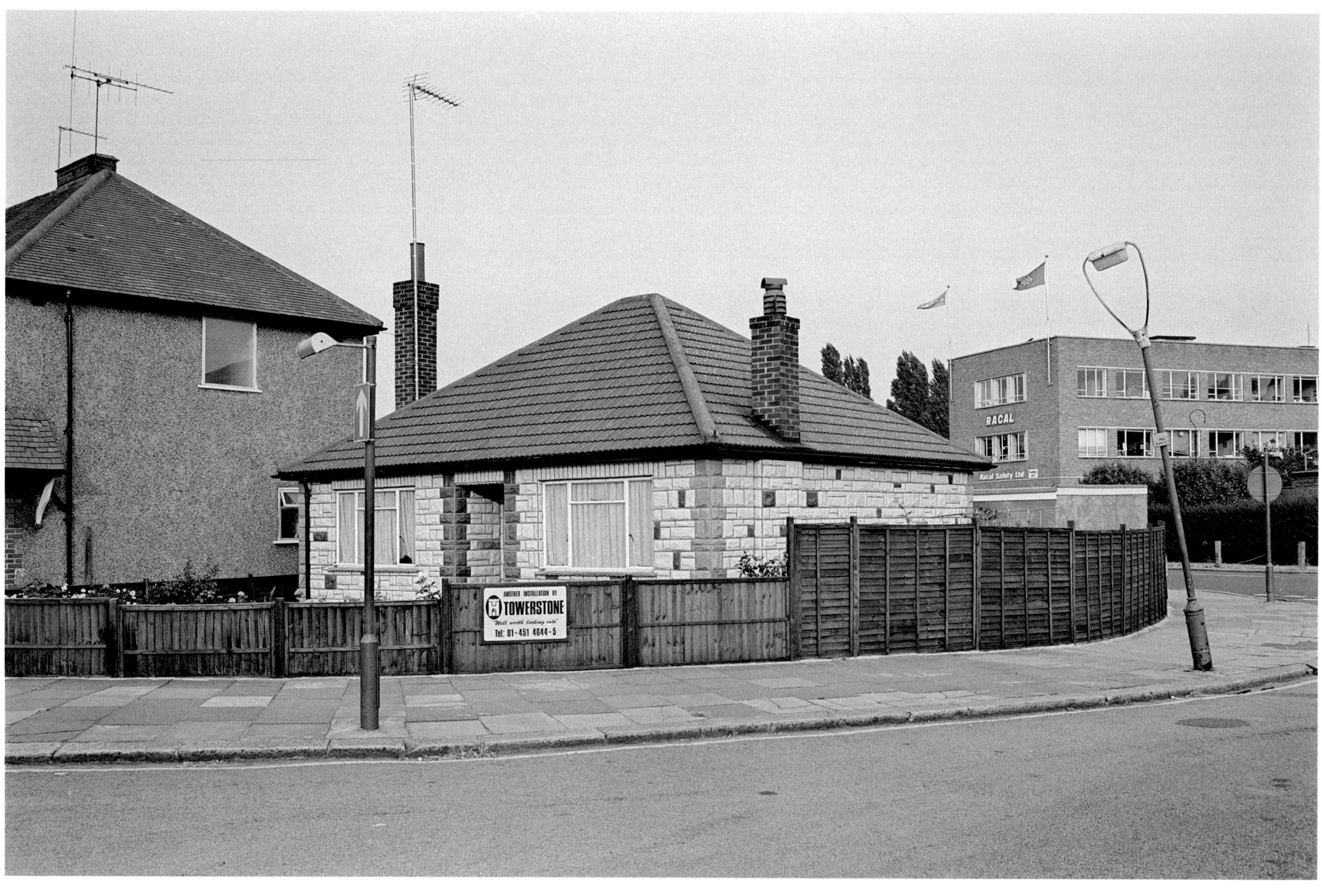

     Wembley, 1983

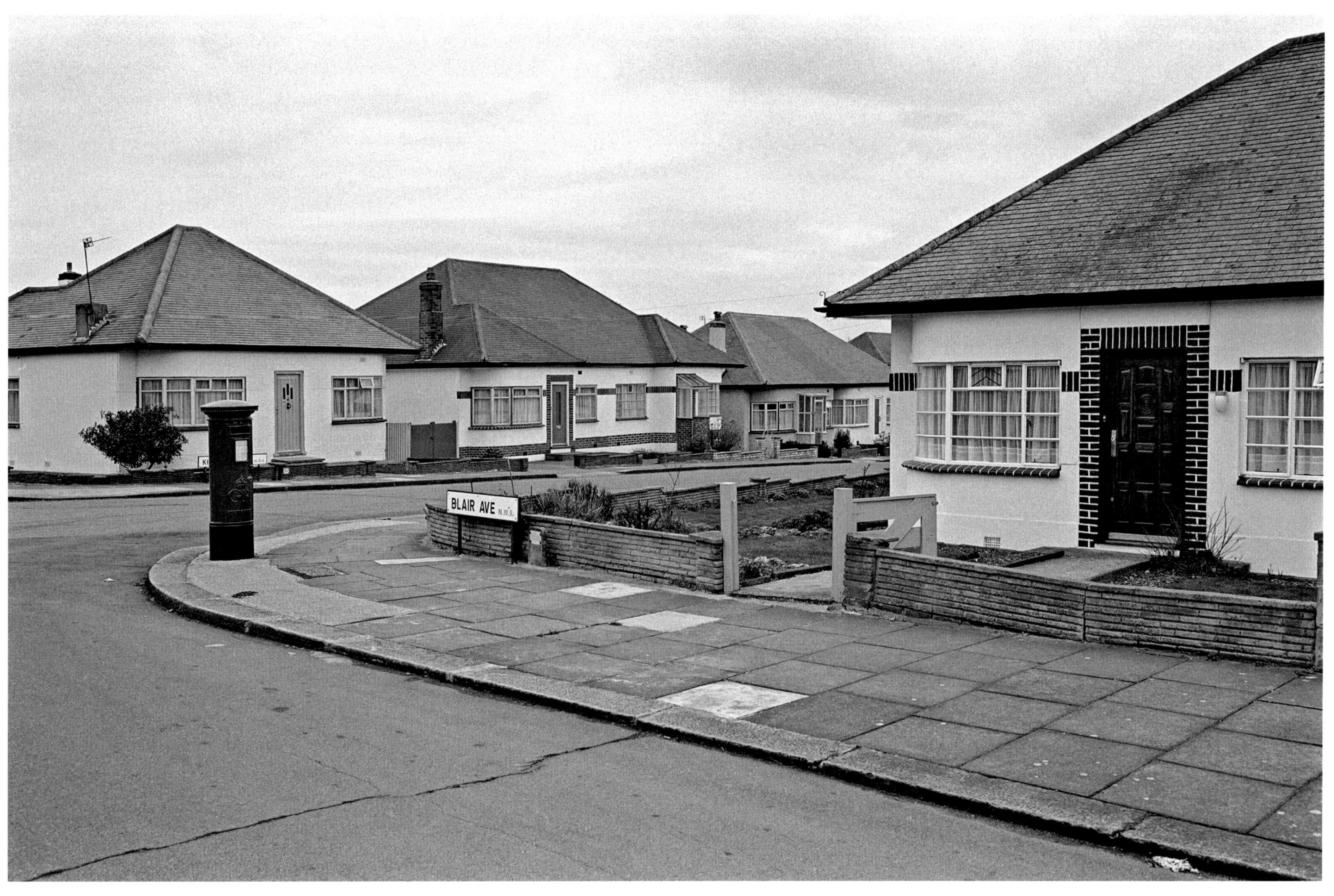

Brent, 1983

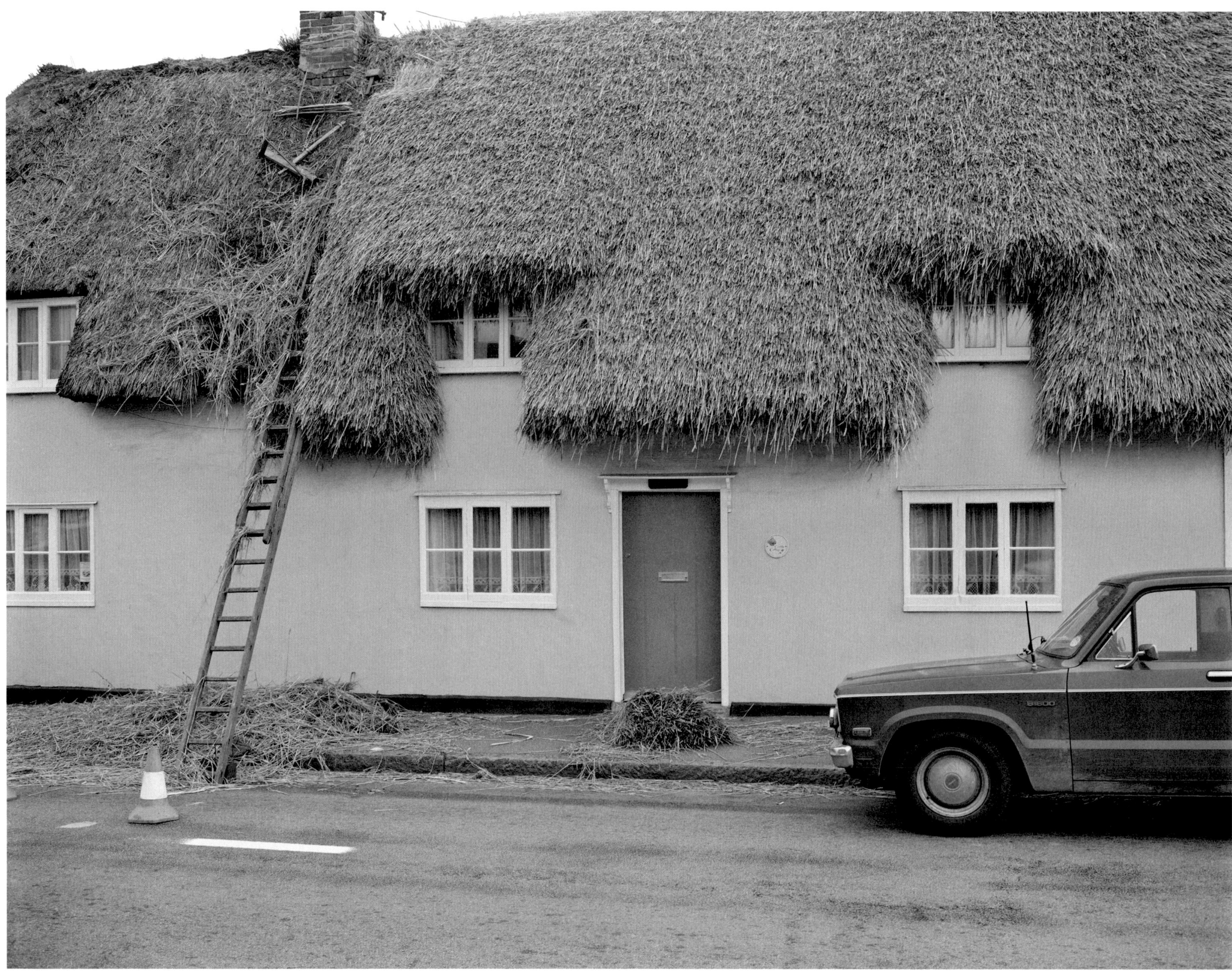

   Suffolk, 1985

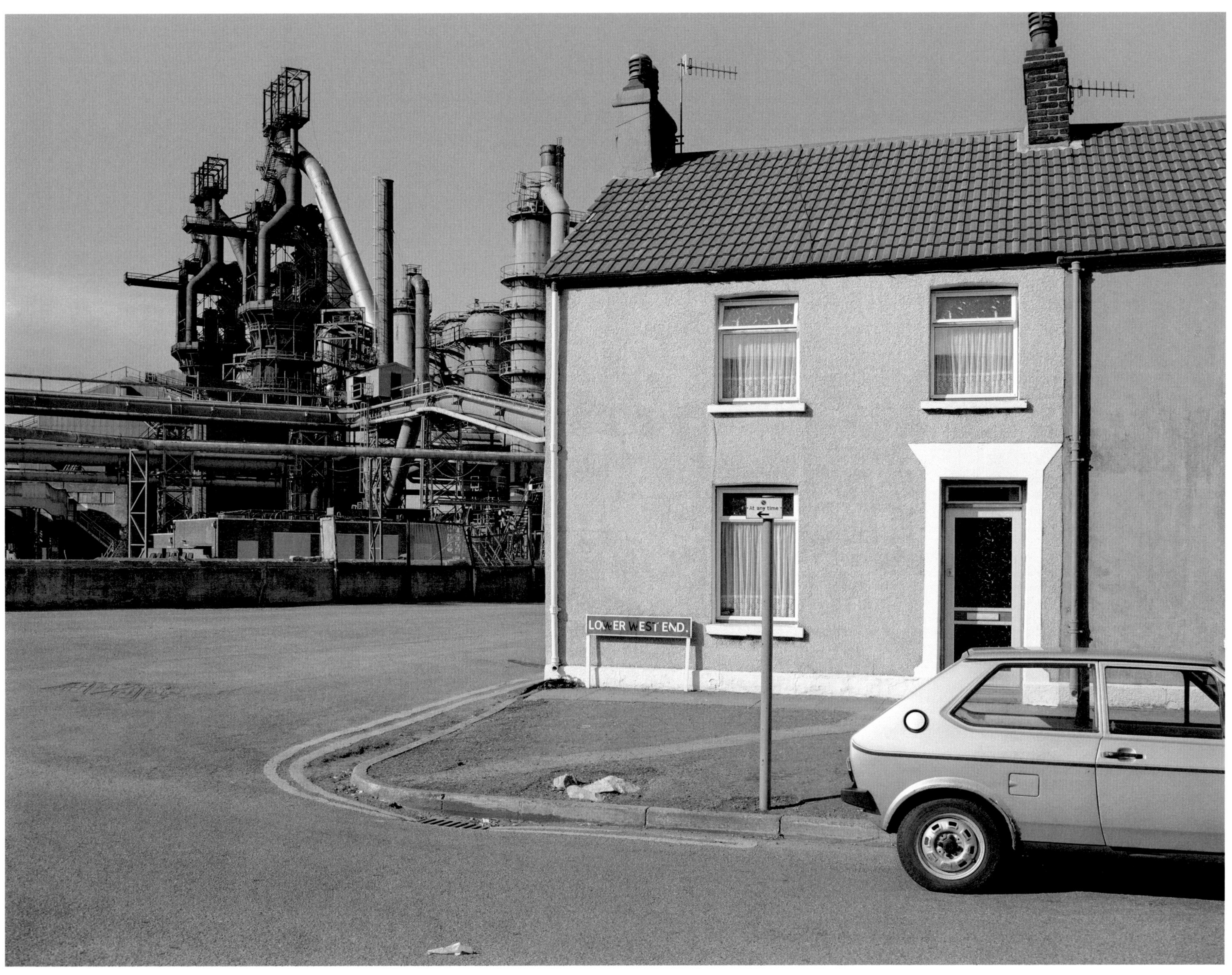

Port Talbot, 1988

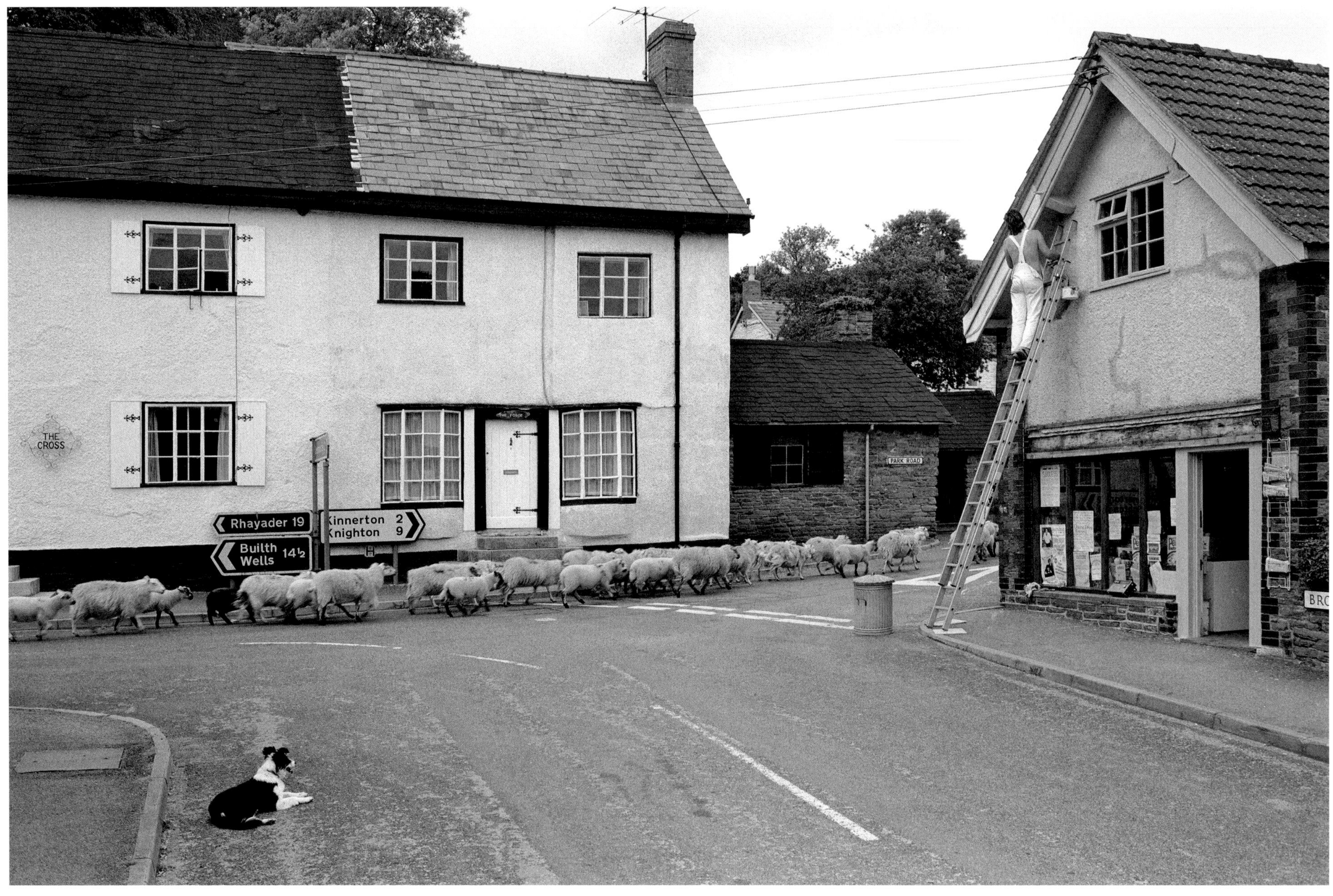

　　　New Radnor, 1987

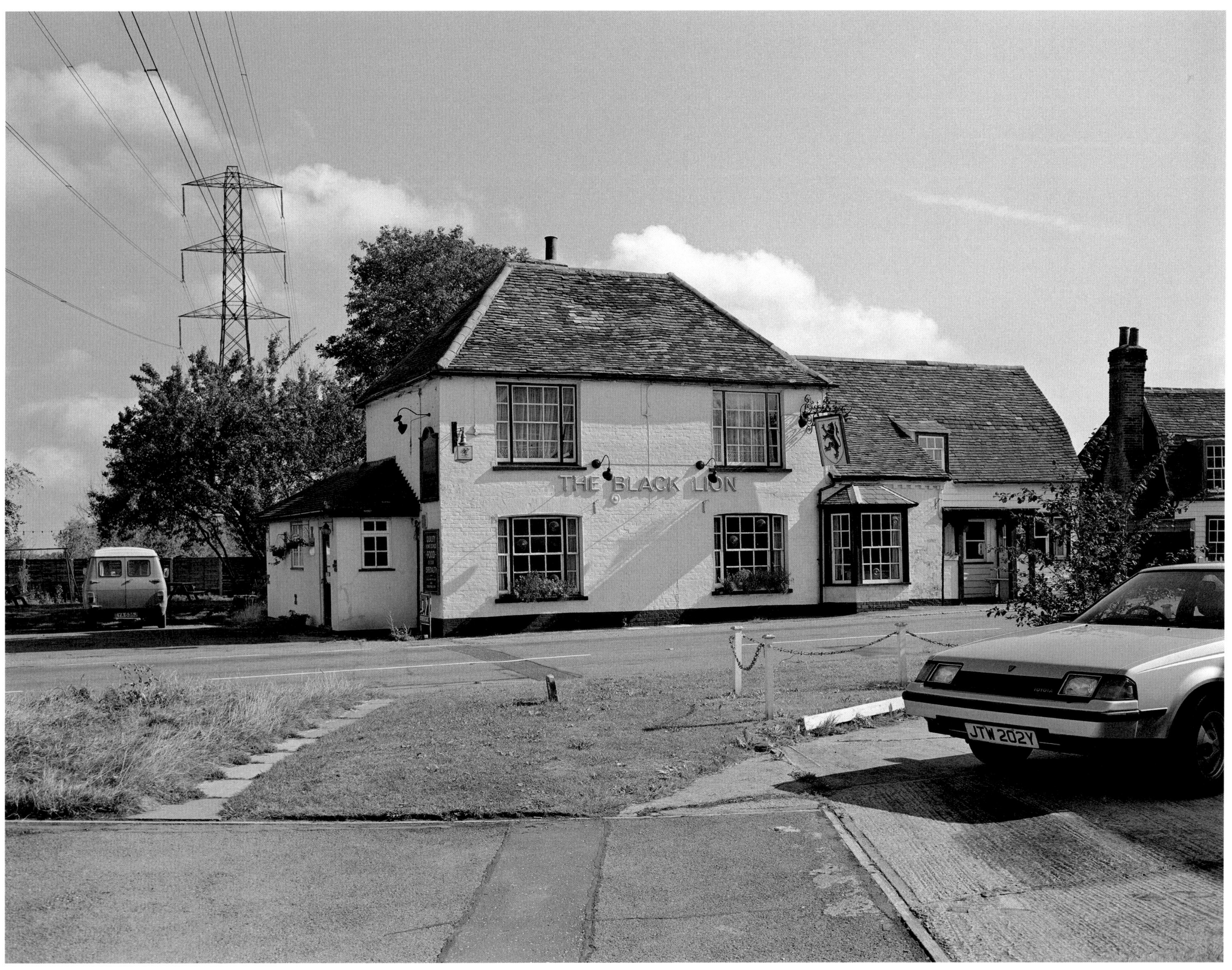

Wiltshire, 1985

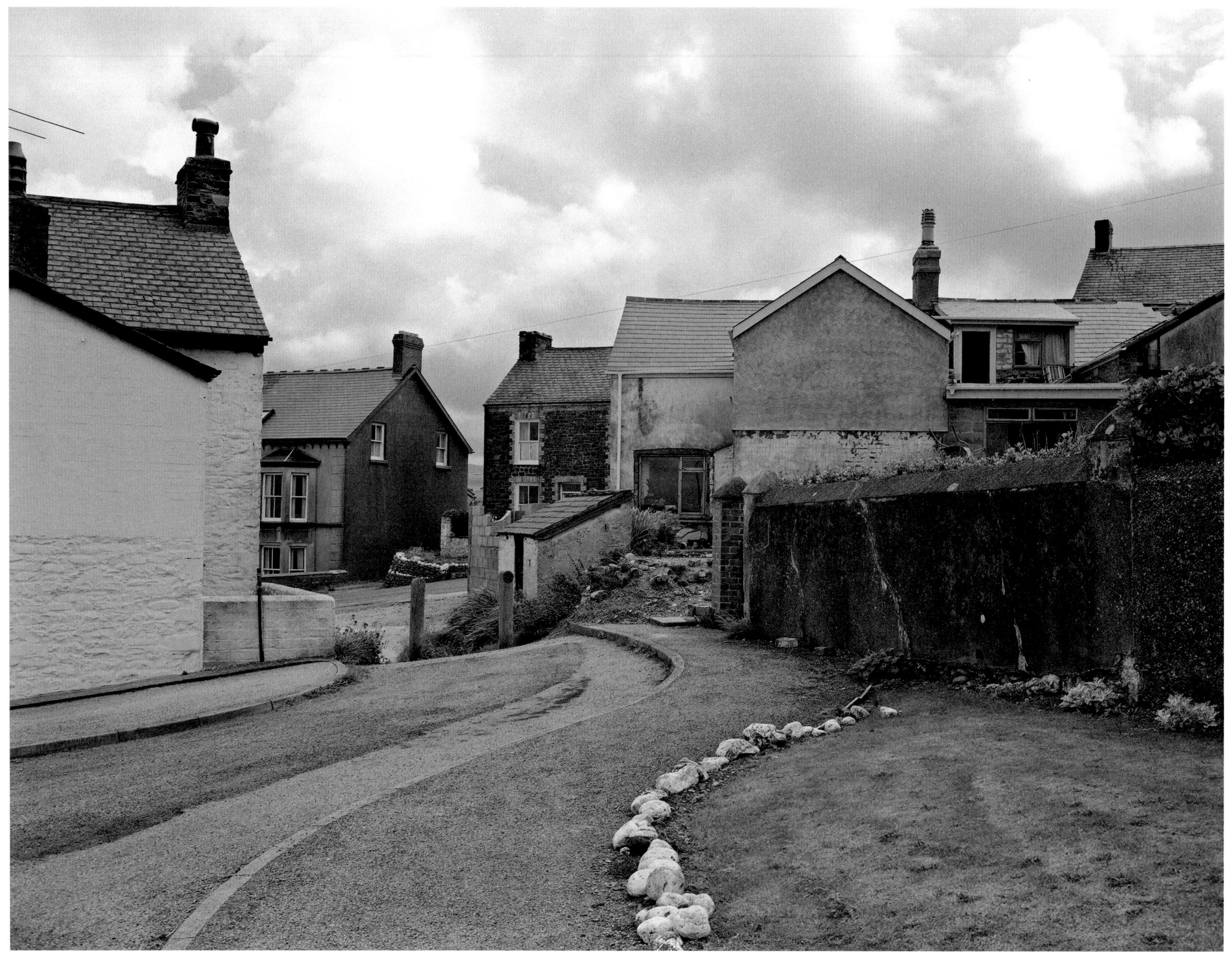

          Borth, 1988

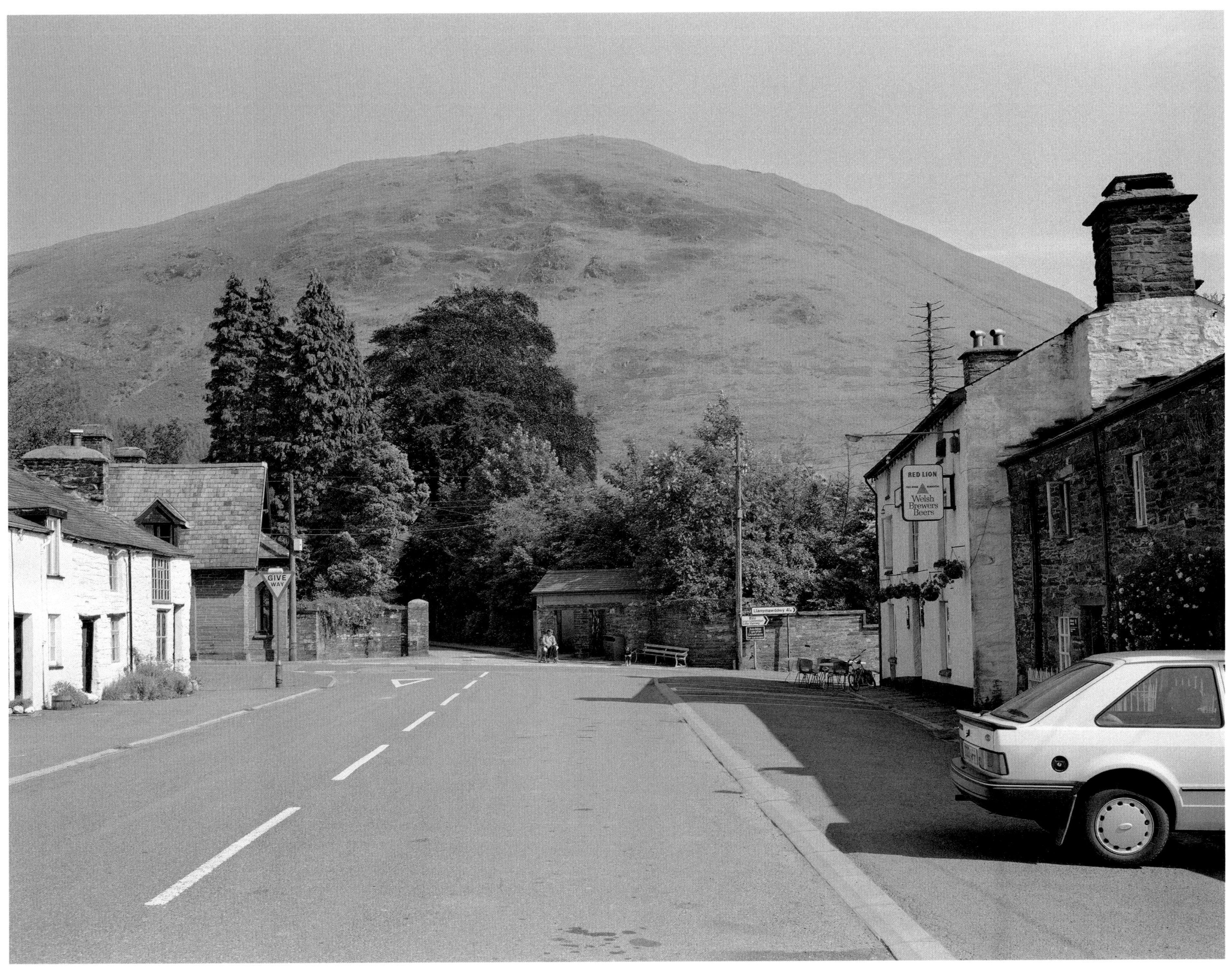

Dinas Mawddwy, 1987

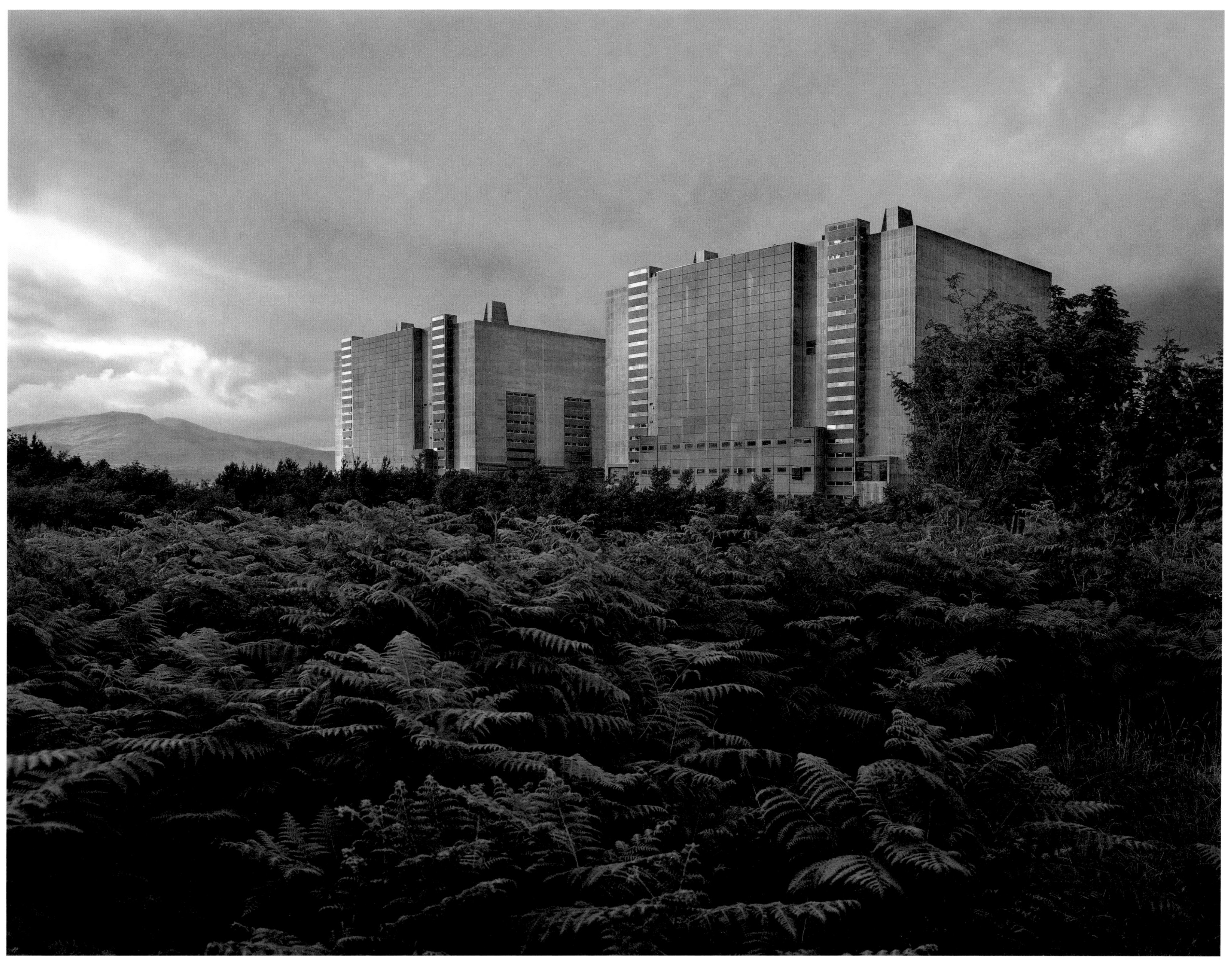

Trawsfynydd, 1987

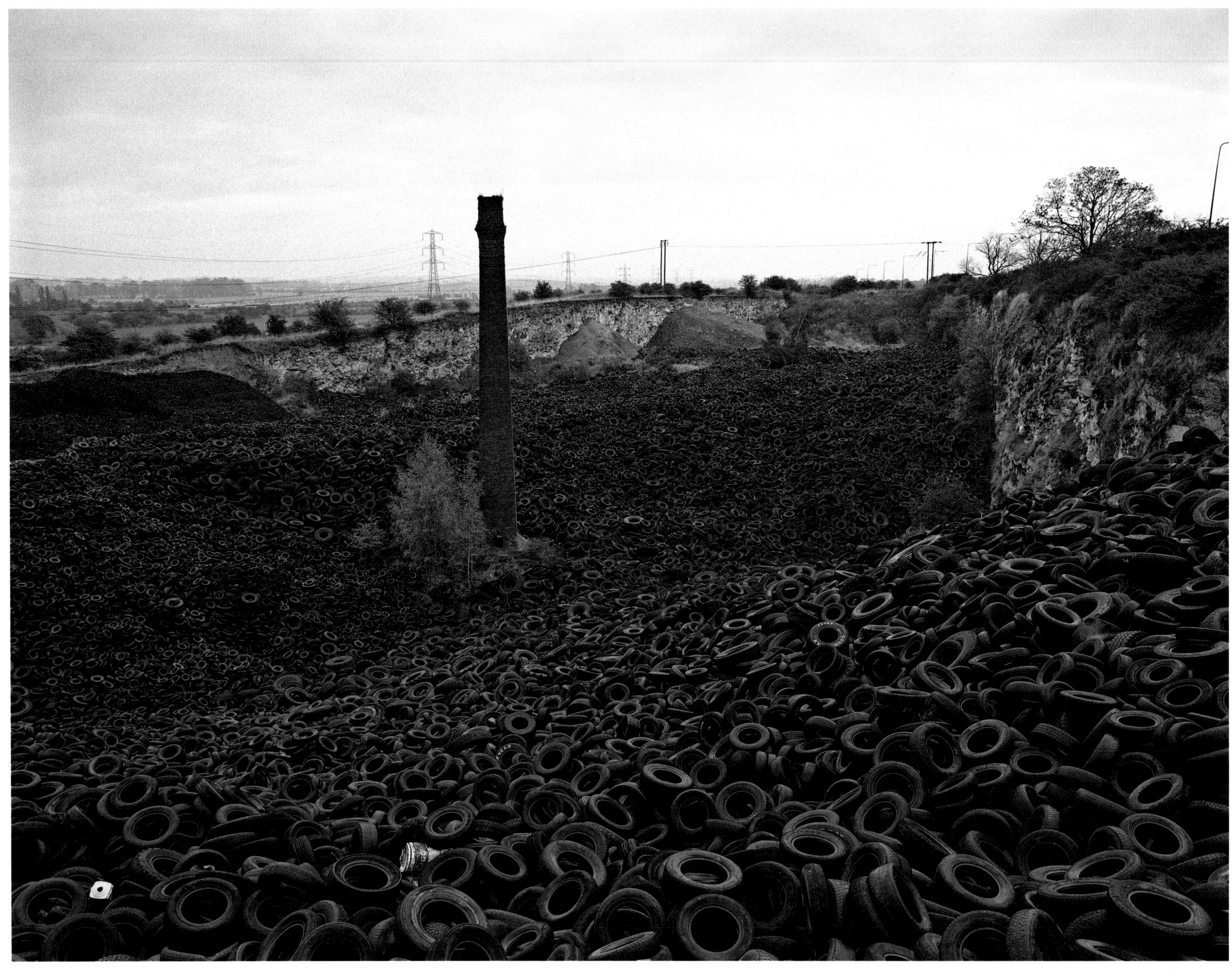

48   Hampole, 1993

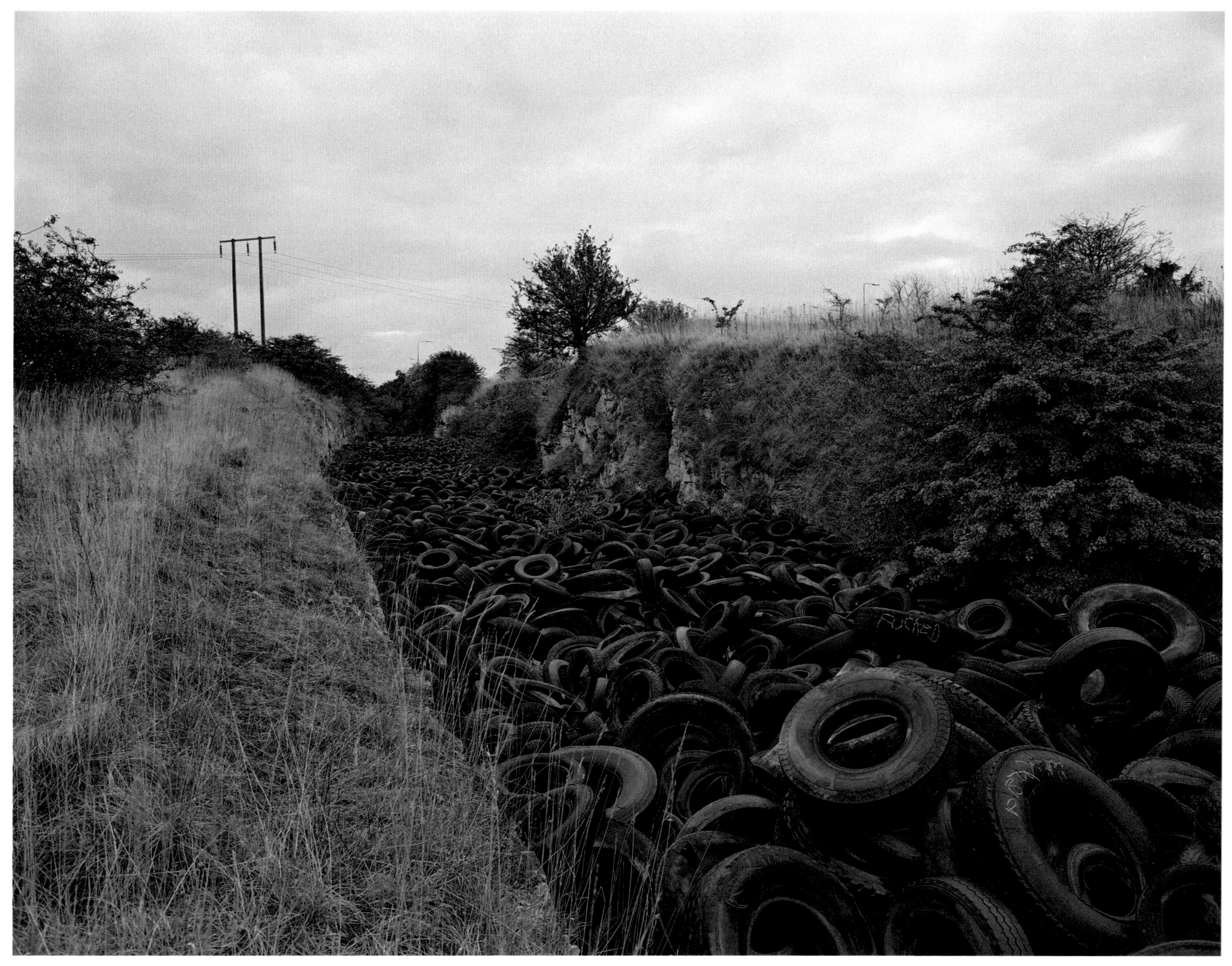

Hampole, 1993

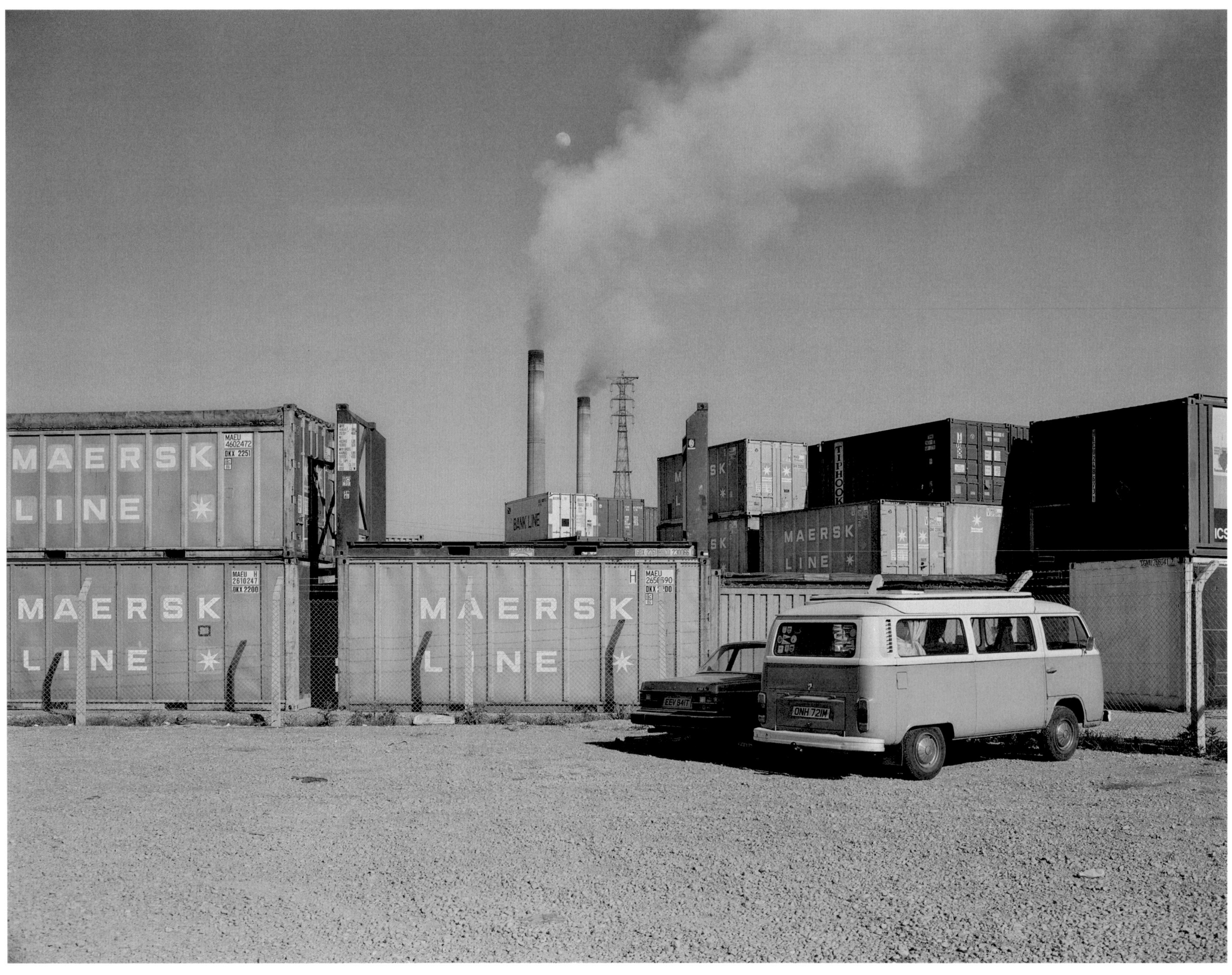

     Tilbury, 1985

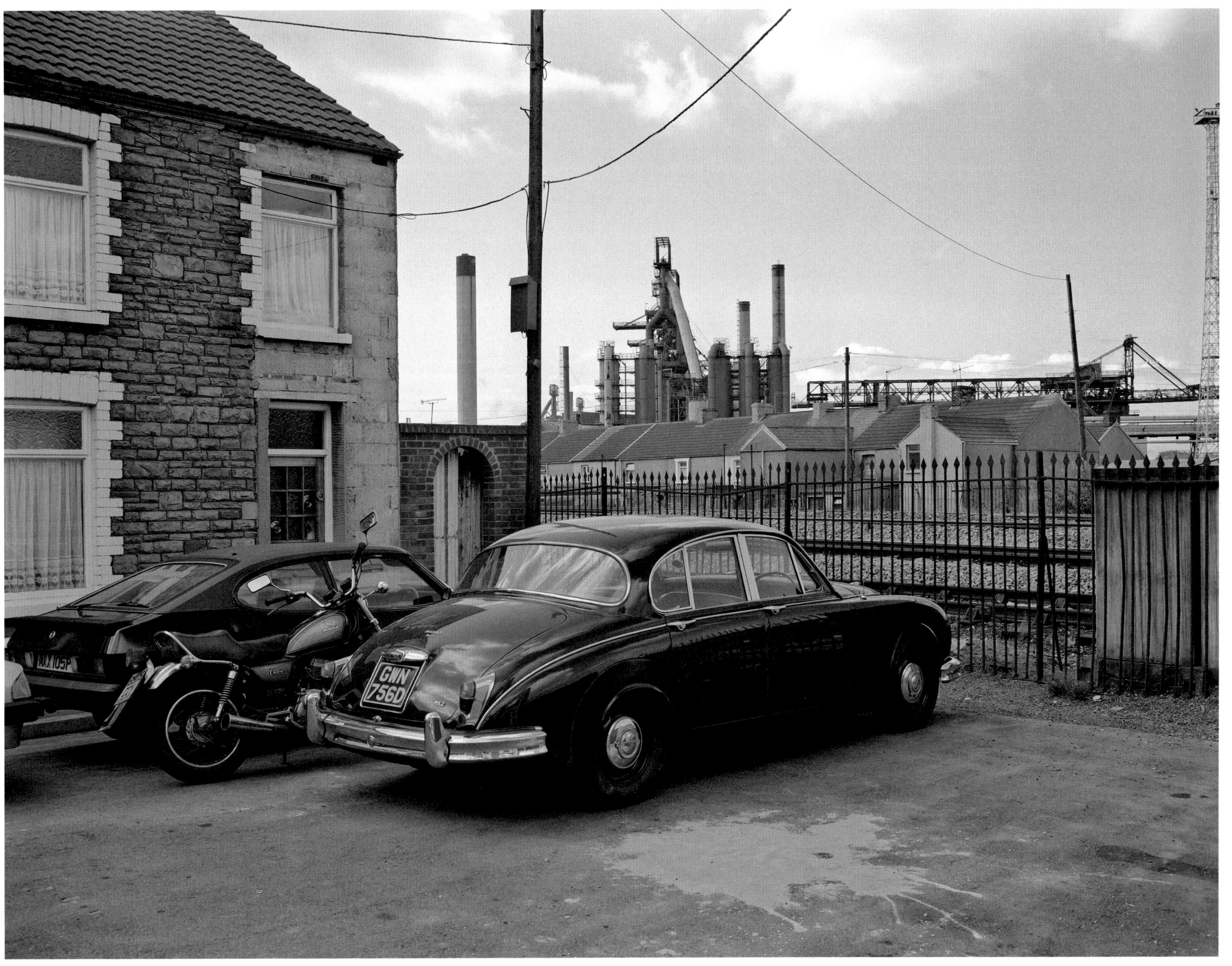

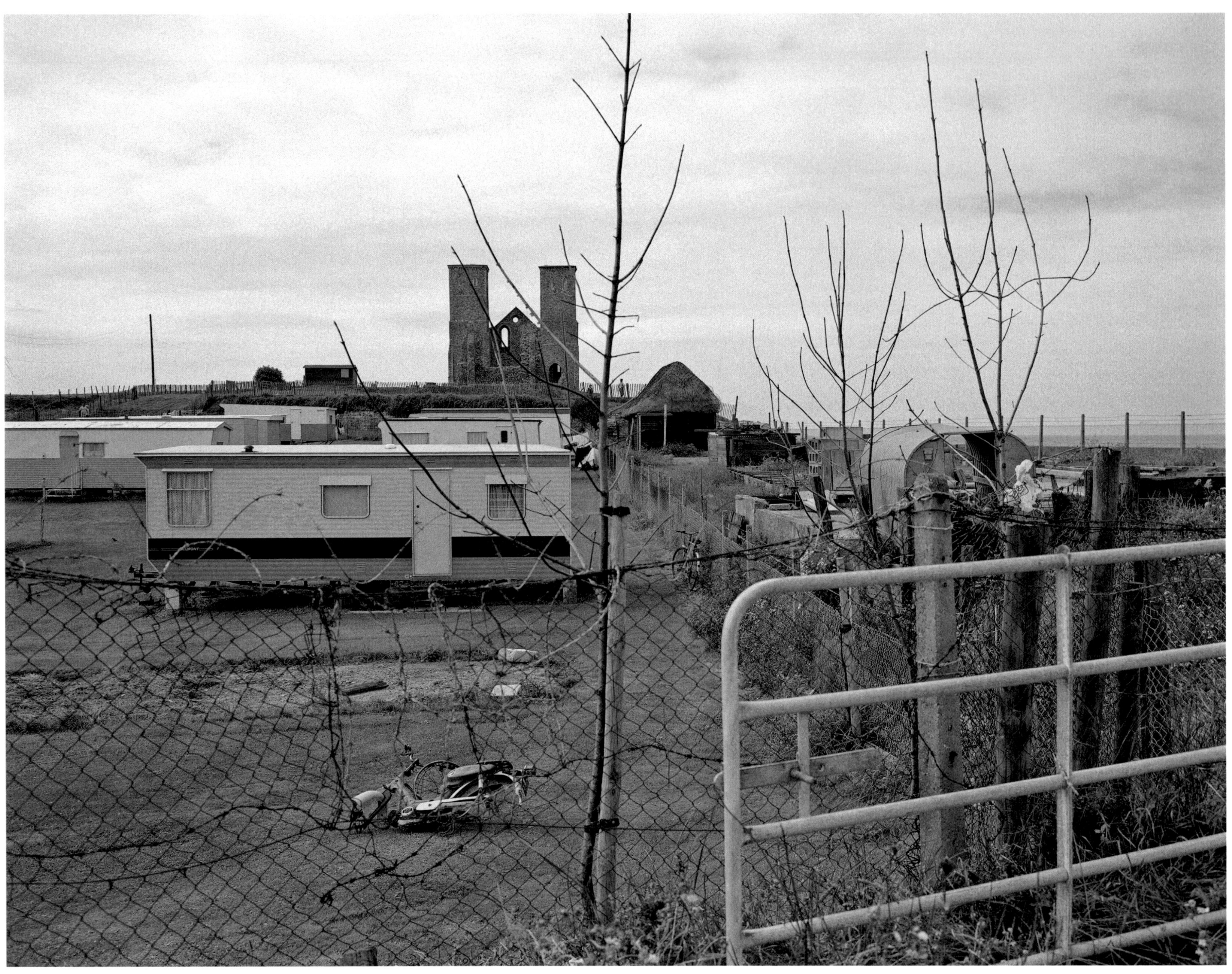

  Reculver Abbey, 1987

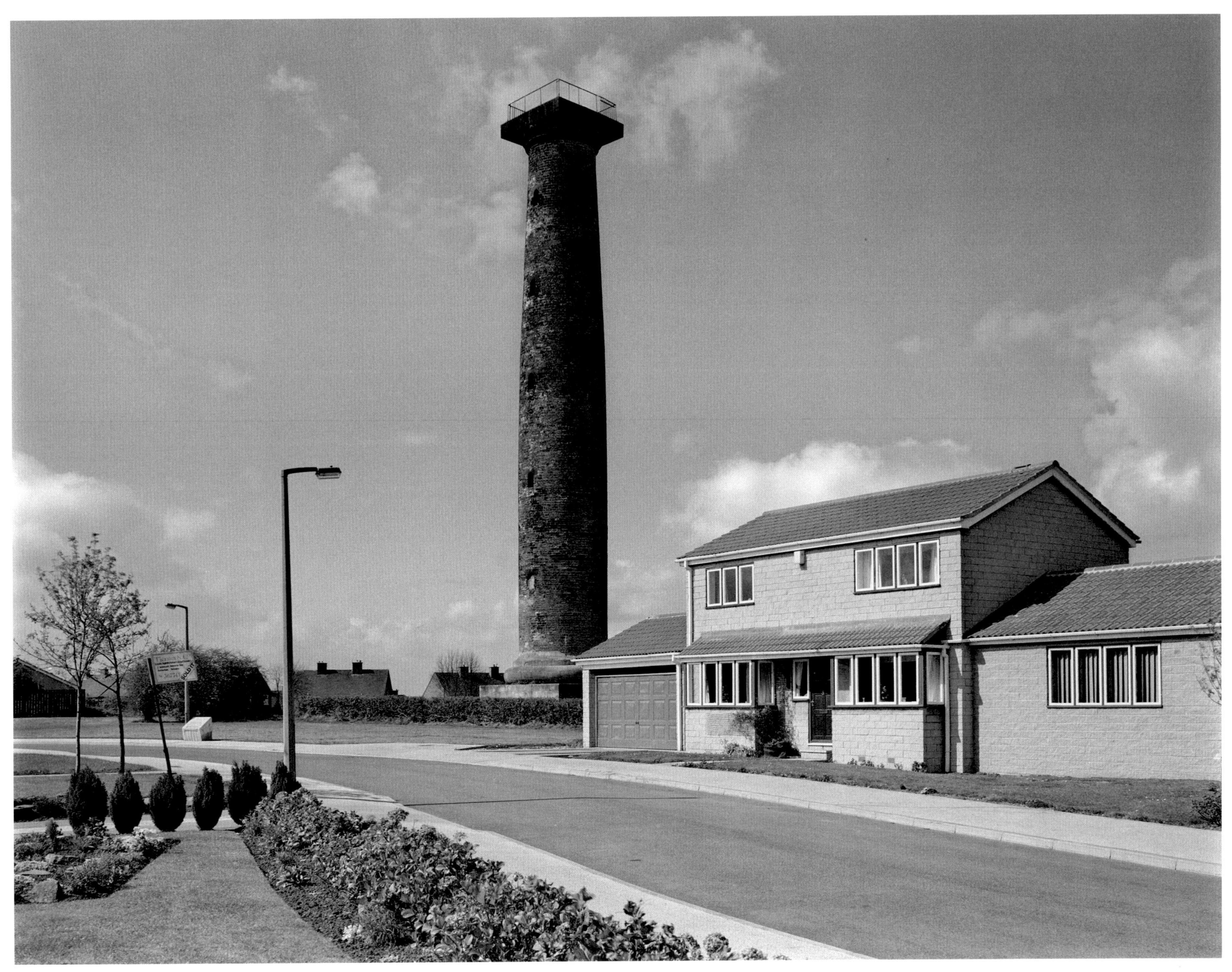

Keppel's Column, 1989   53

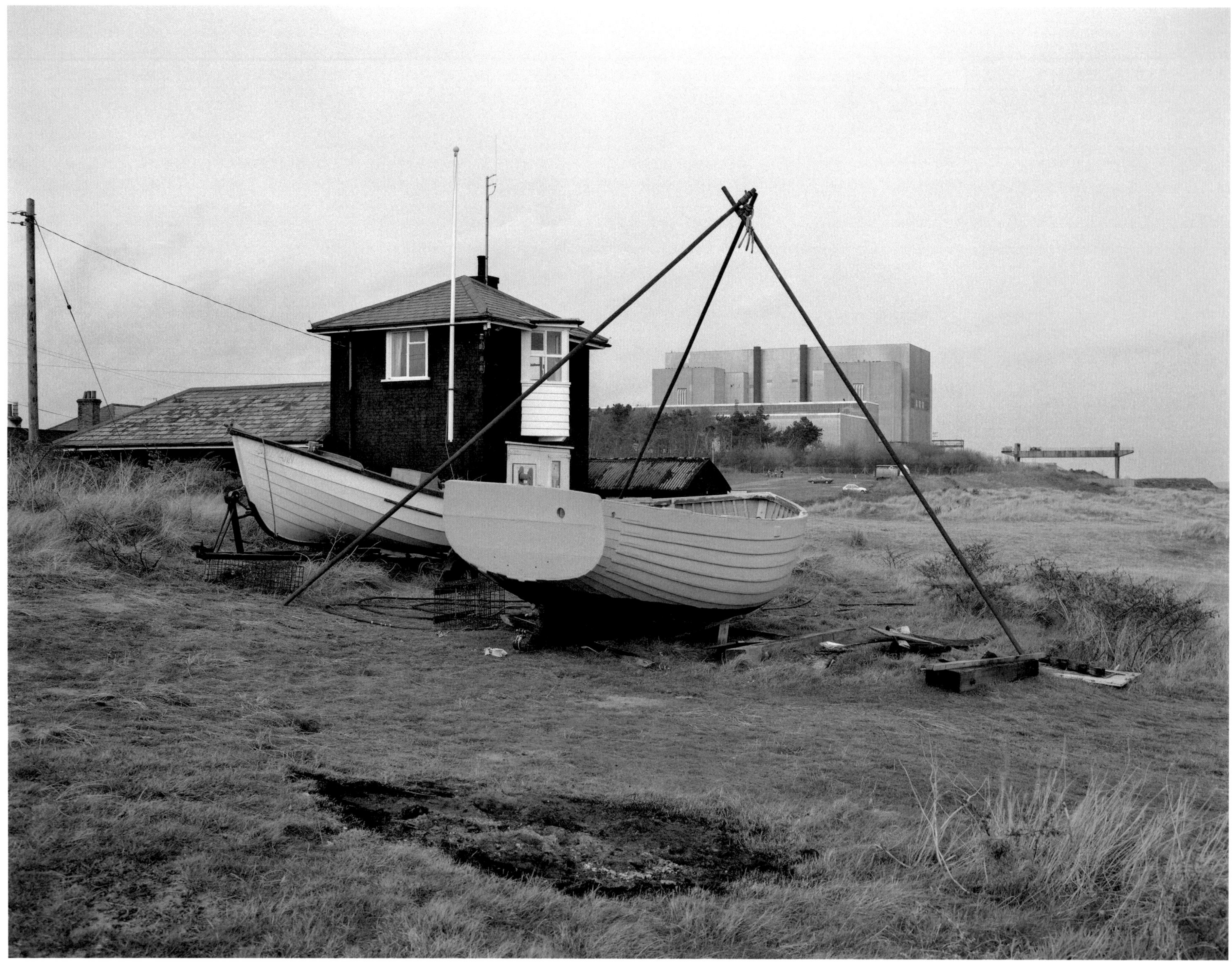

54   Sizewell, 1985

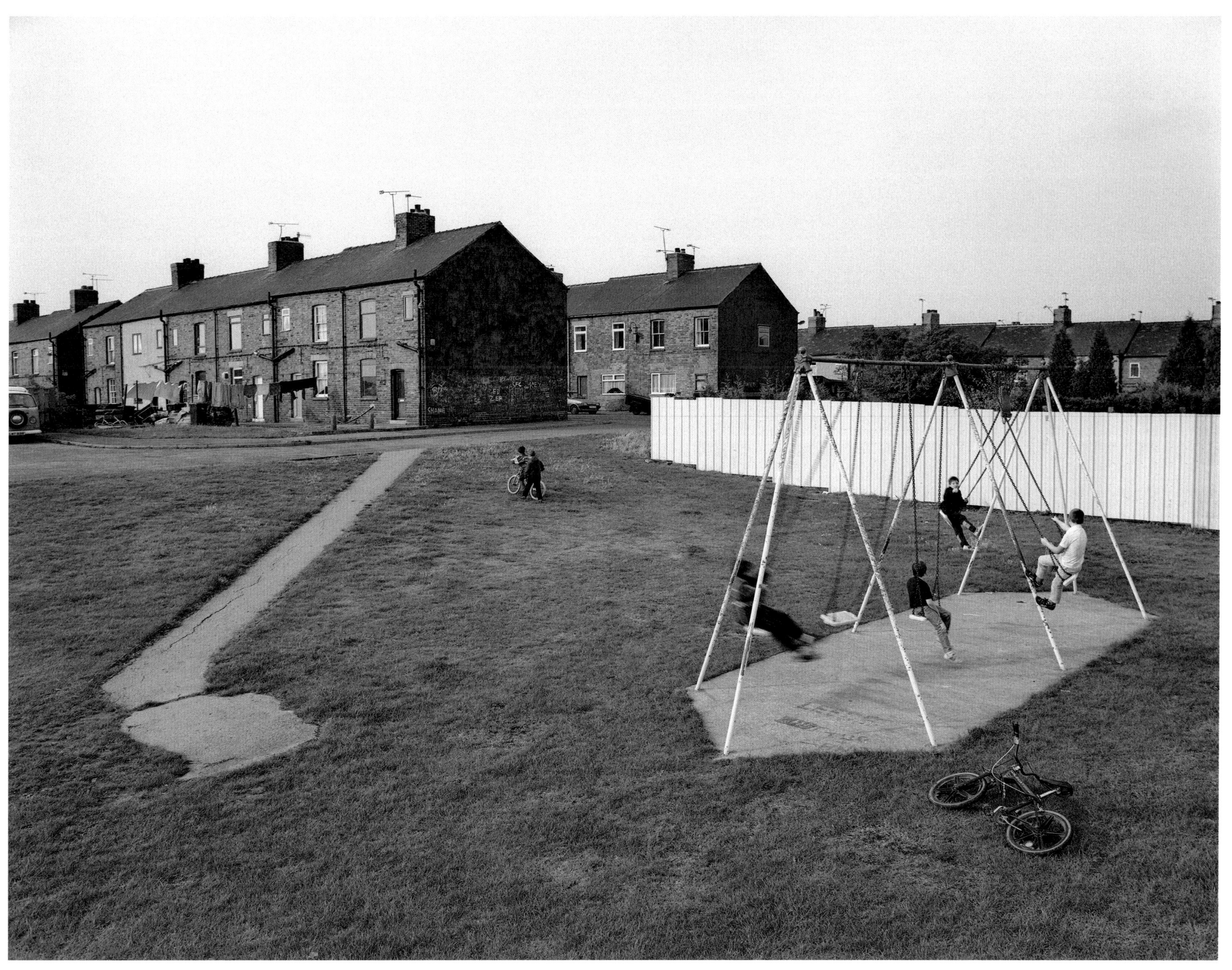

Arkwright Town, 1990

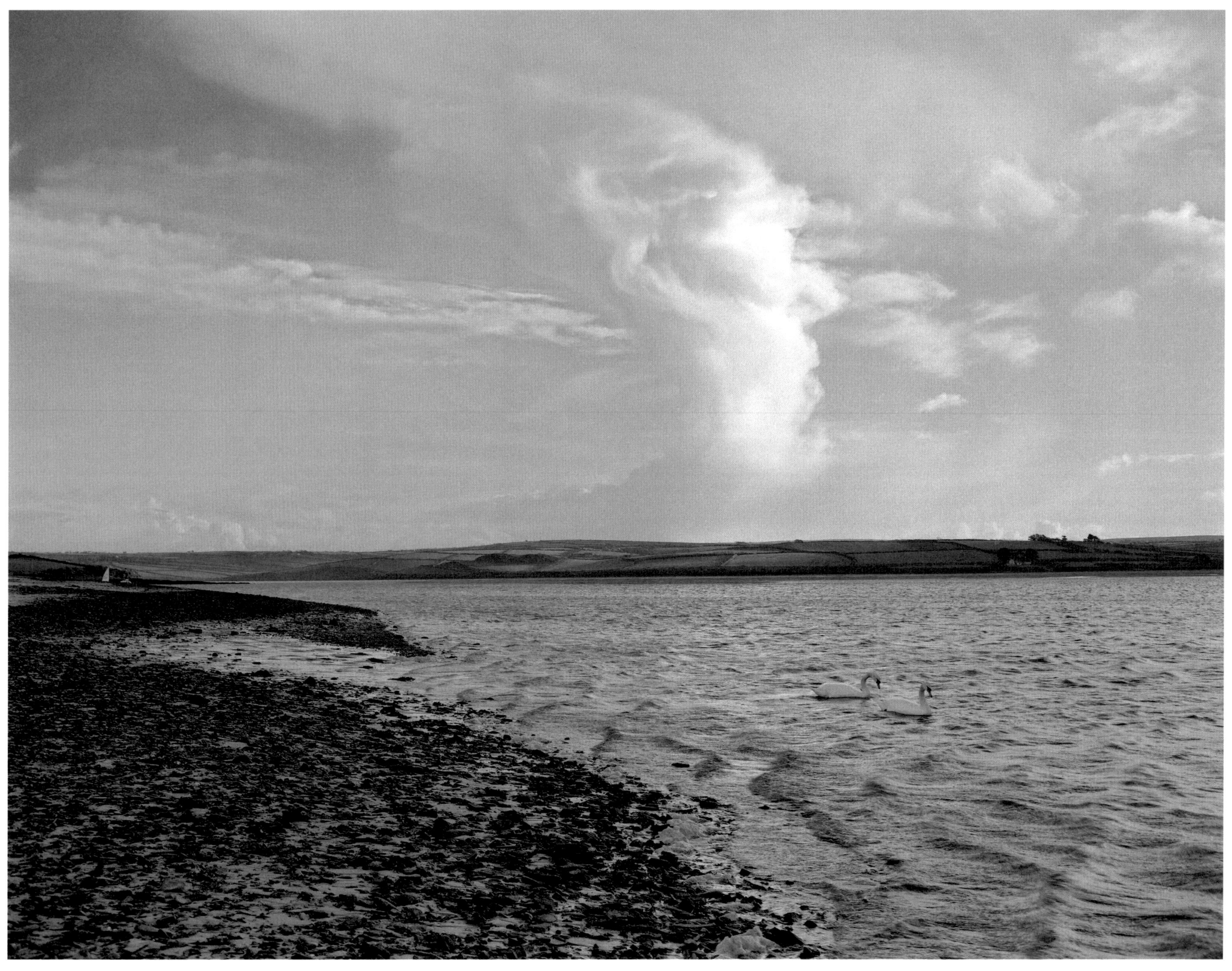

Cornwall, 1985

     Devon, 1989

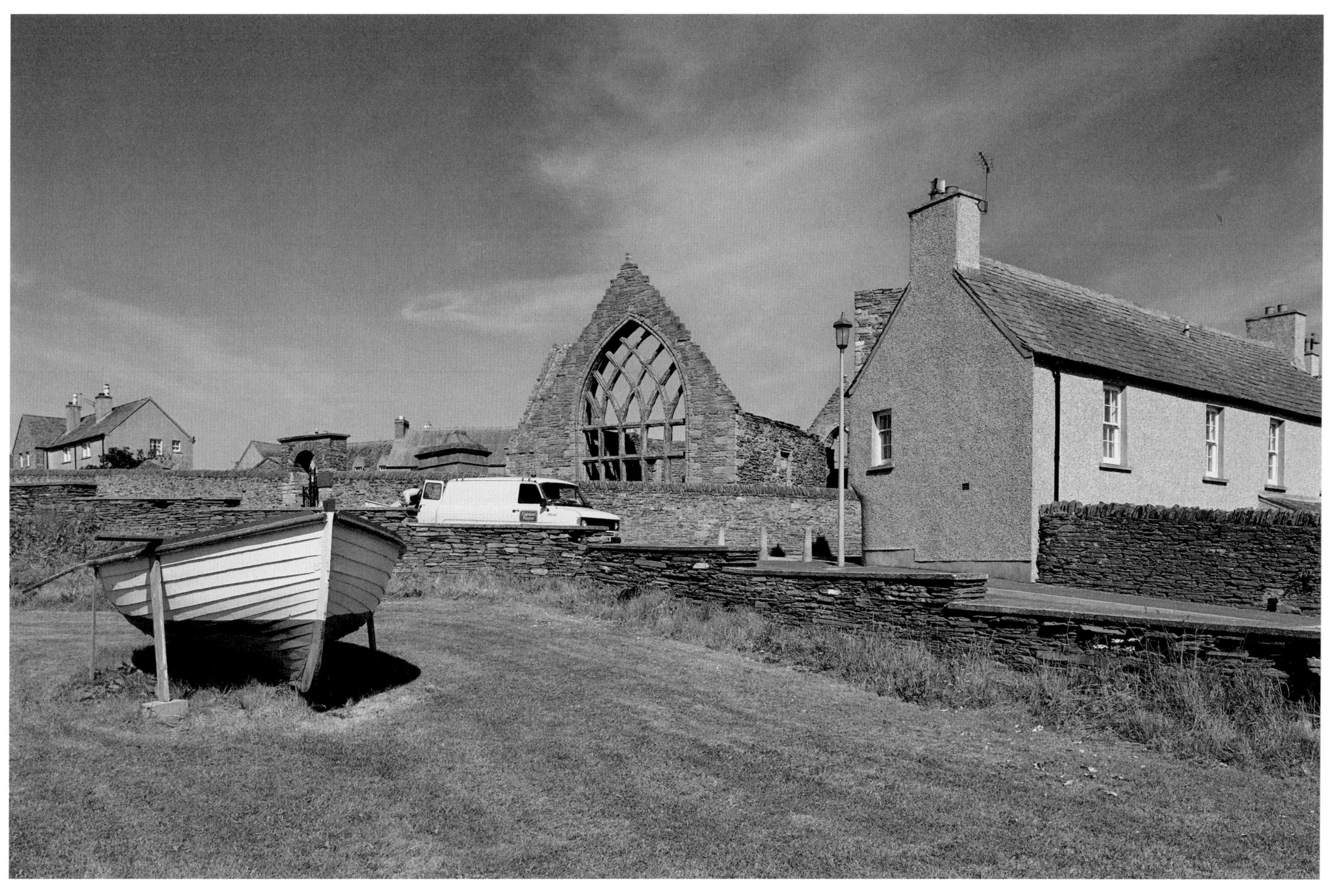

Thurso, 1984

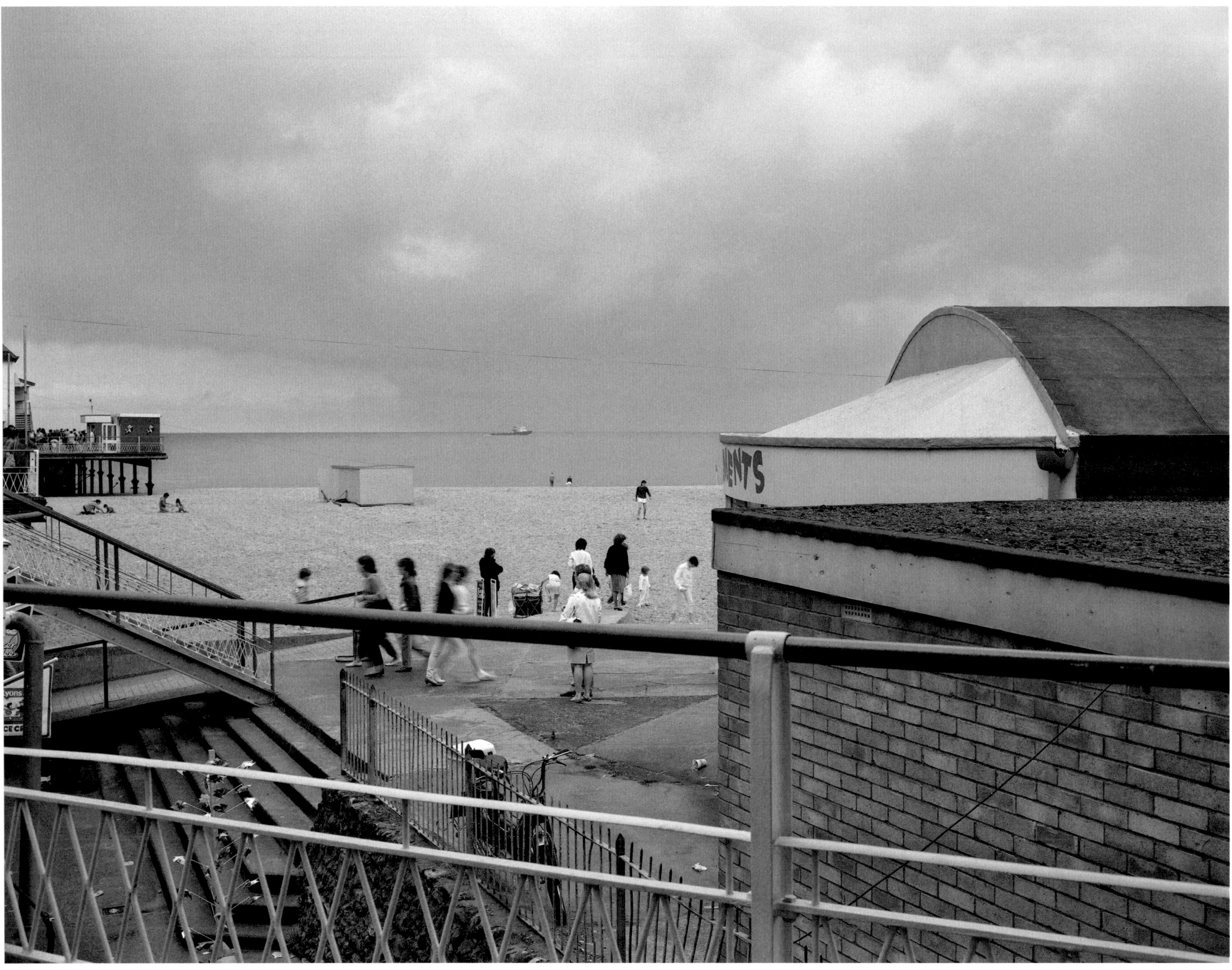

60   Great Yarmouth, 1985

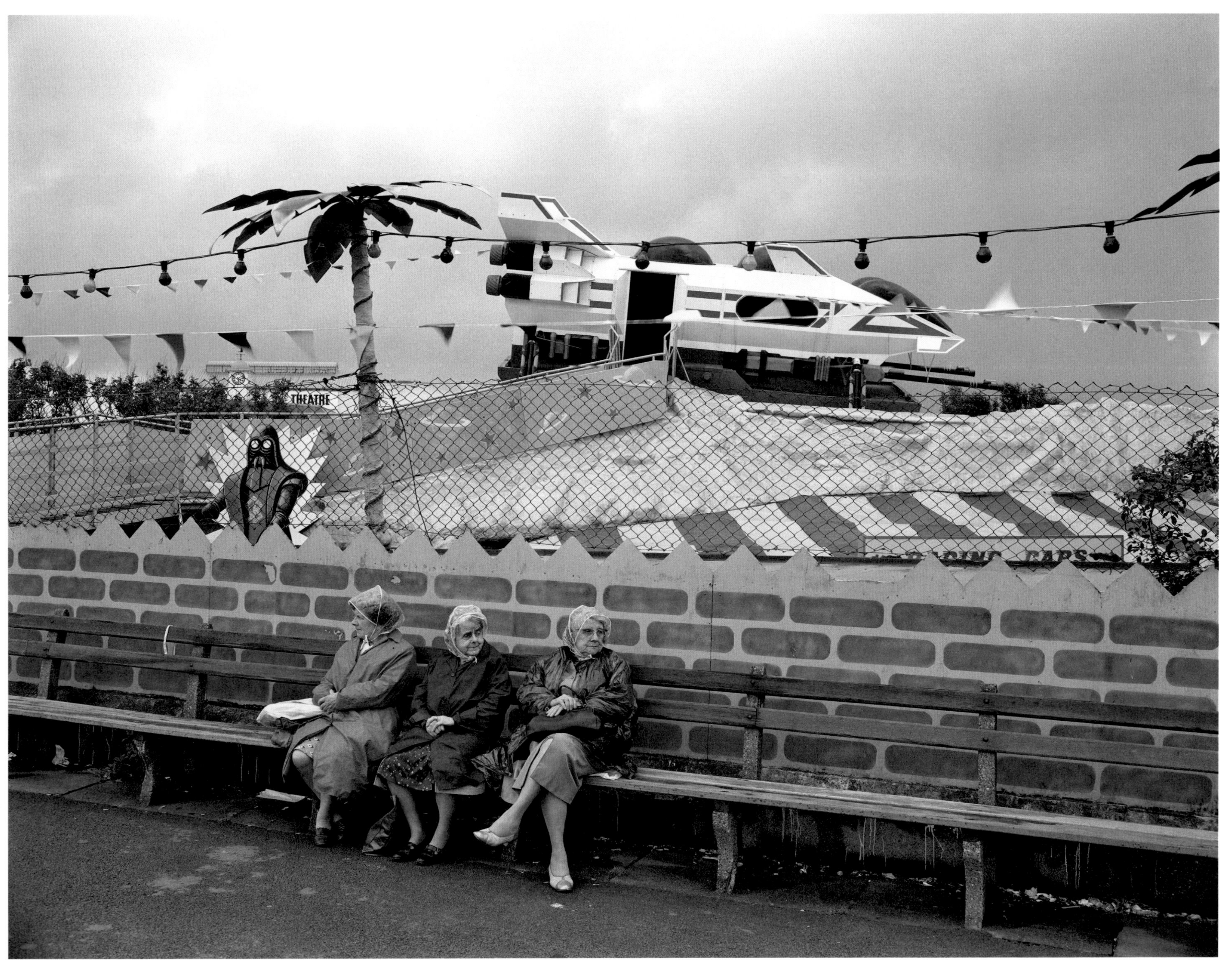

Great Yarmouth, 1985

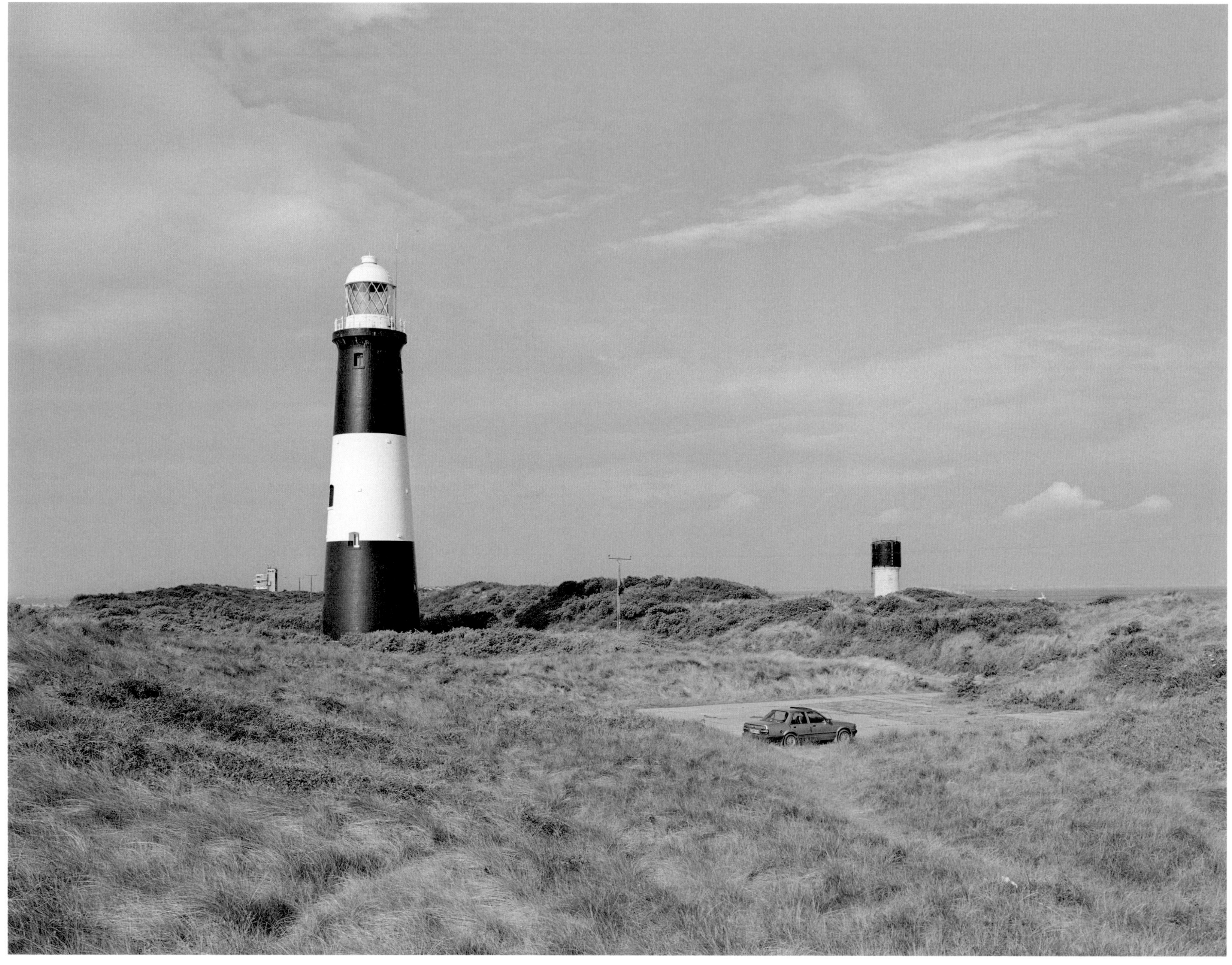

  Spurn, 1990

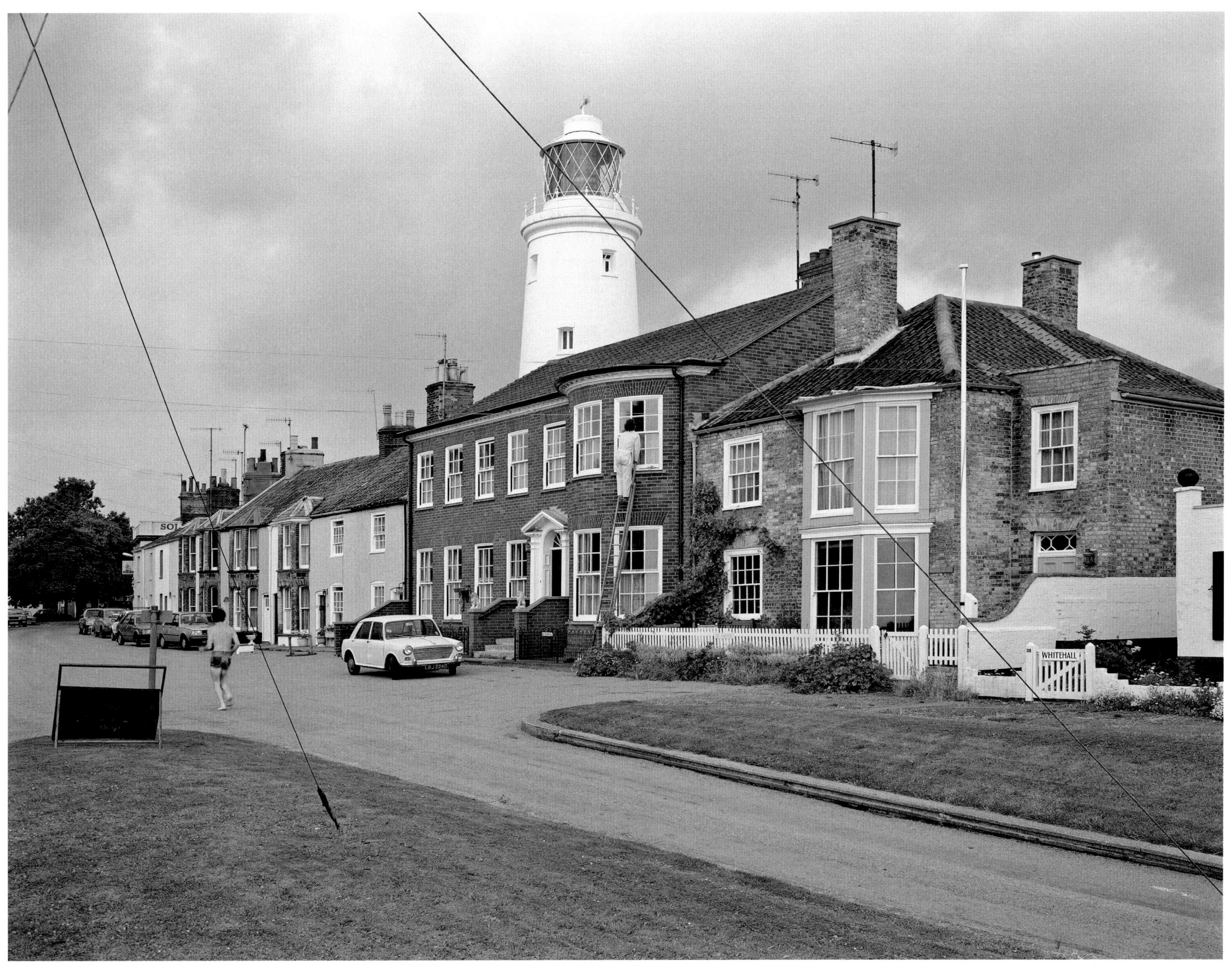

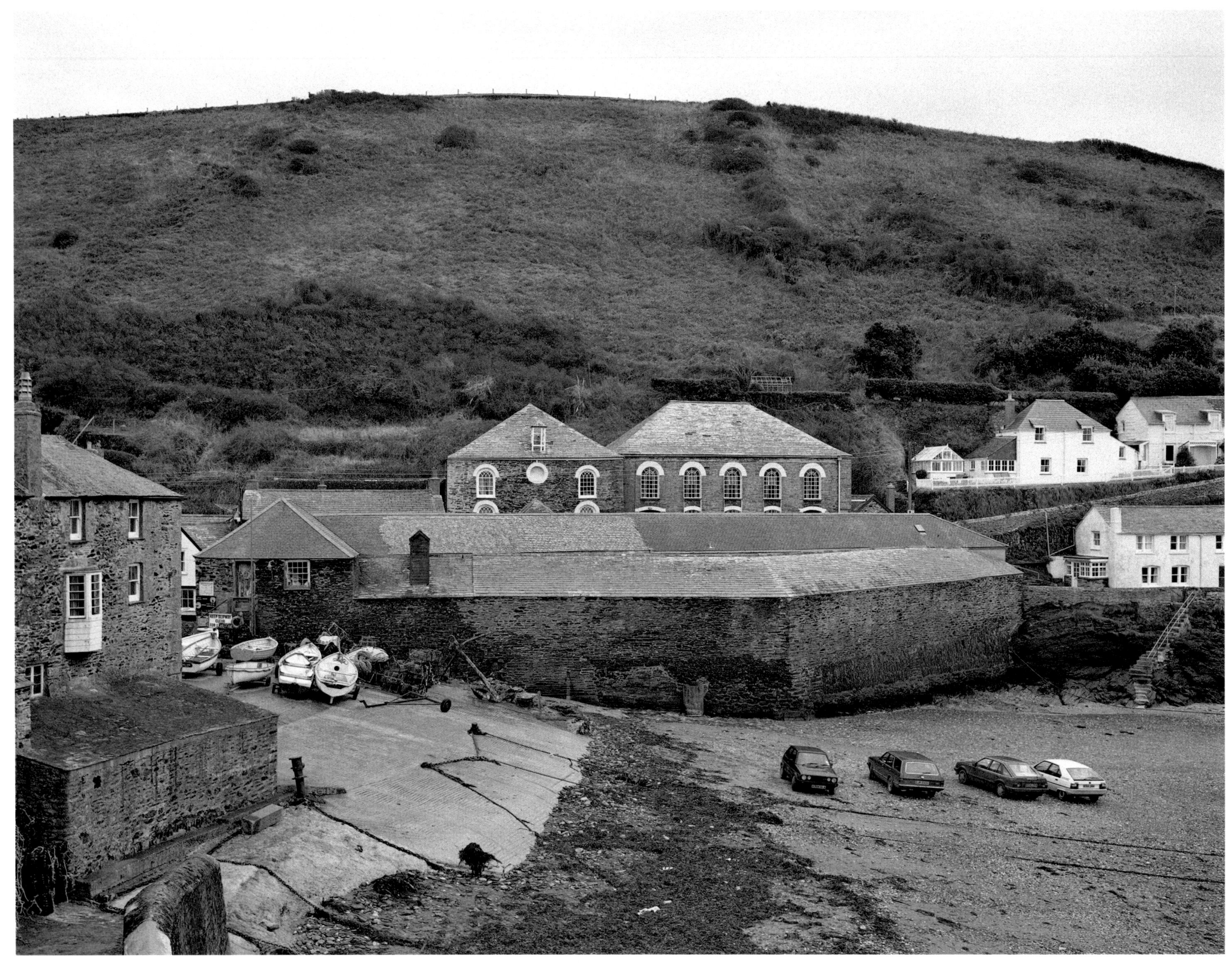

64   Port Isaac, 1996

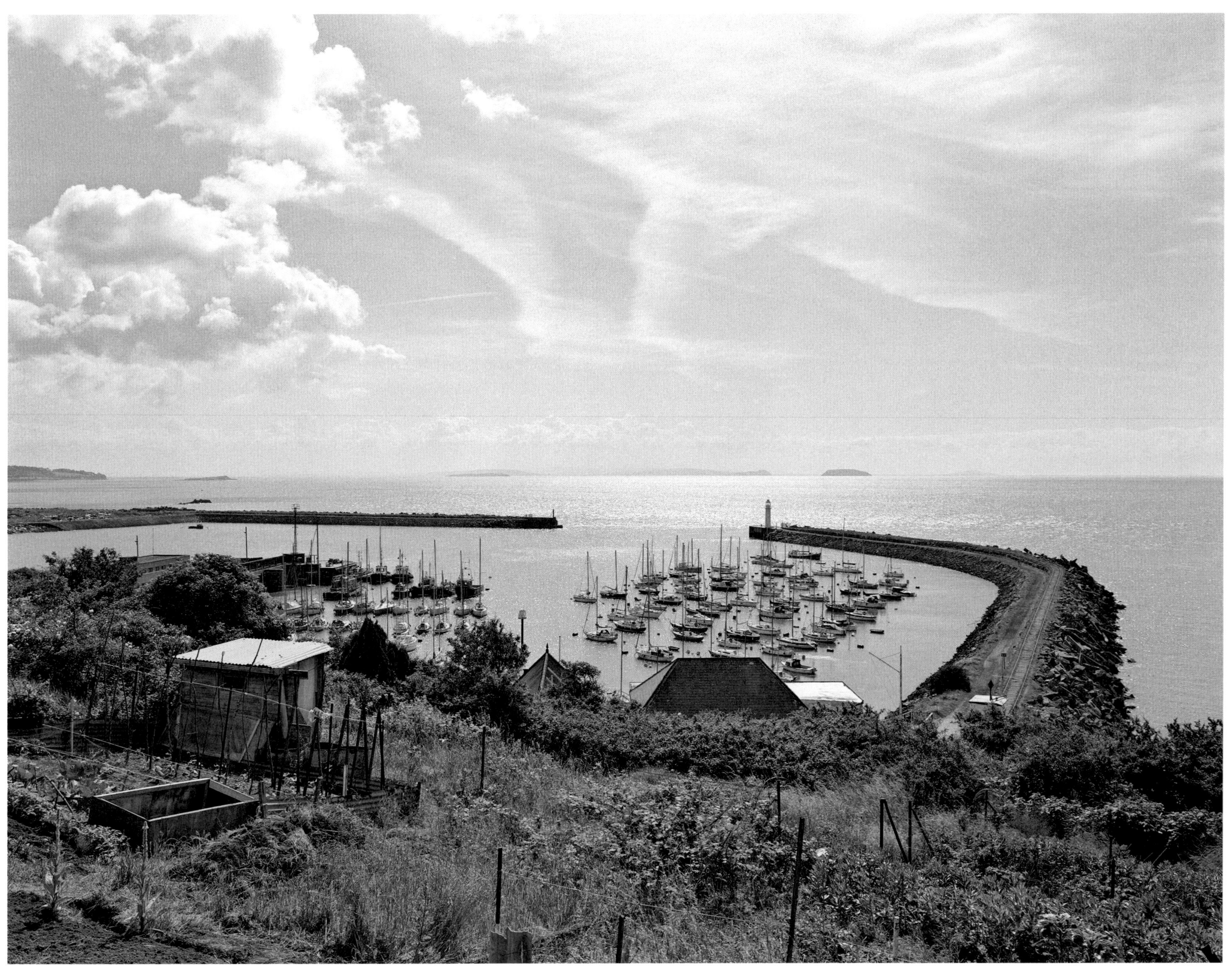

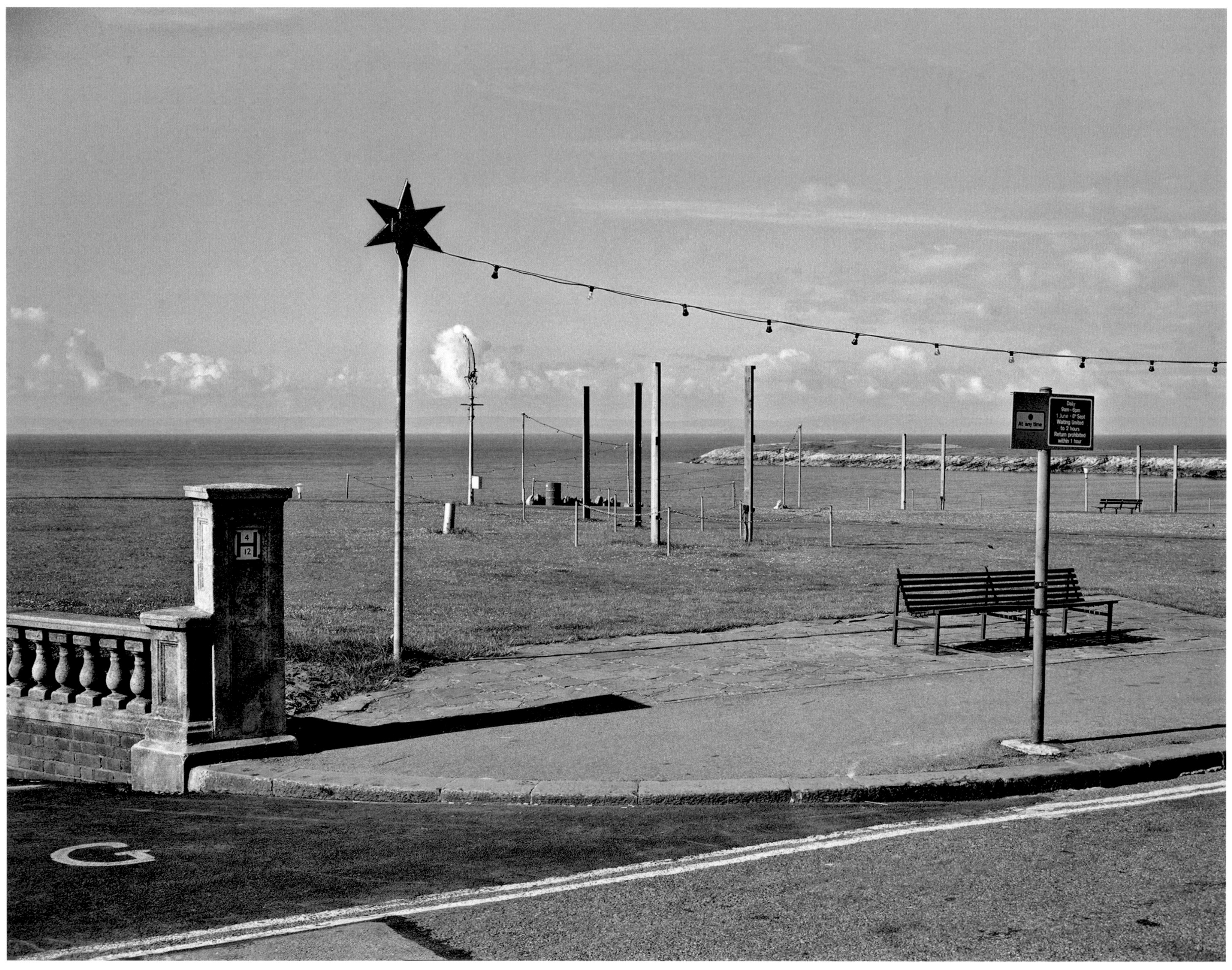

     Barry Island, 1987

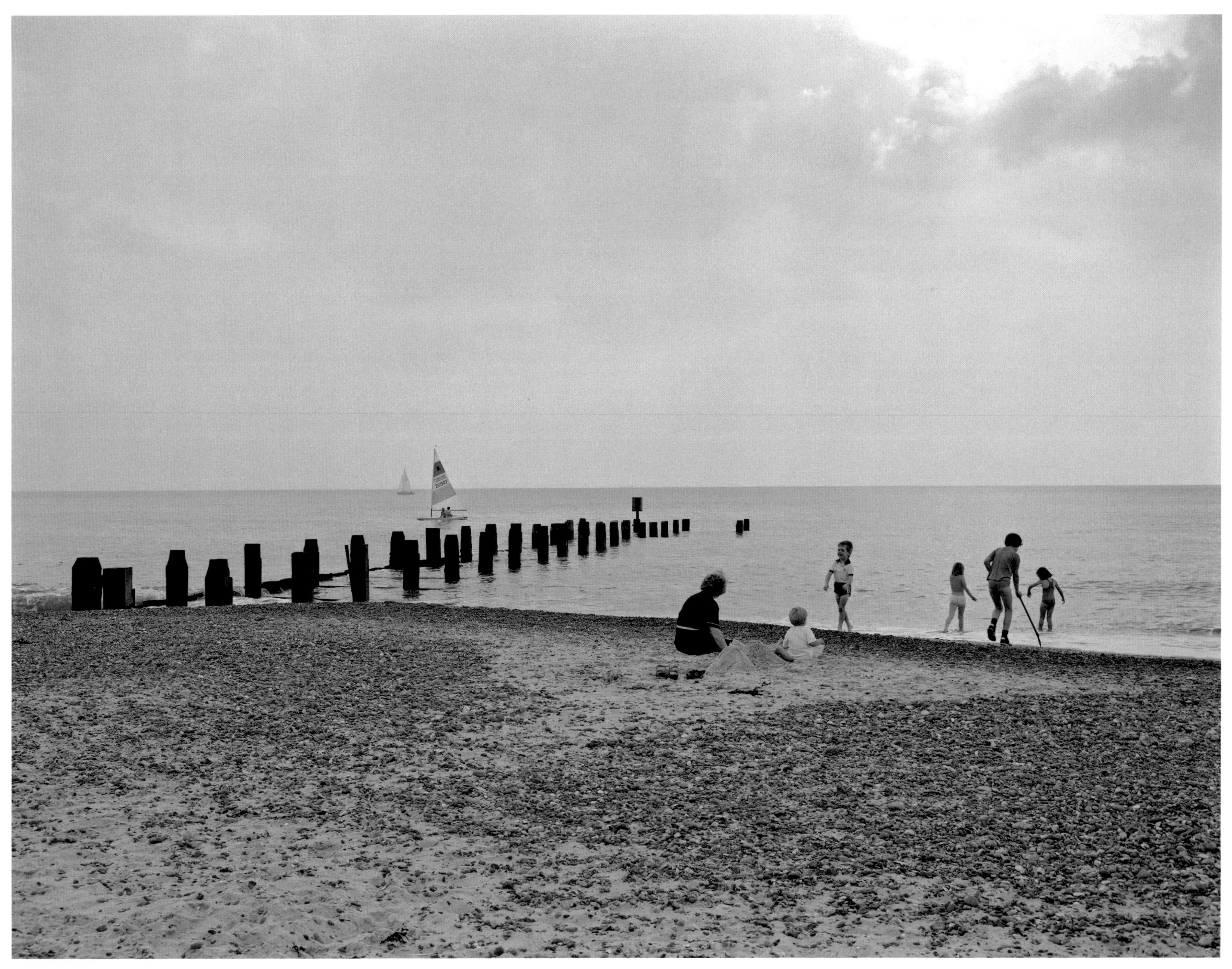

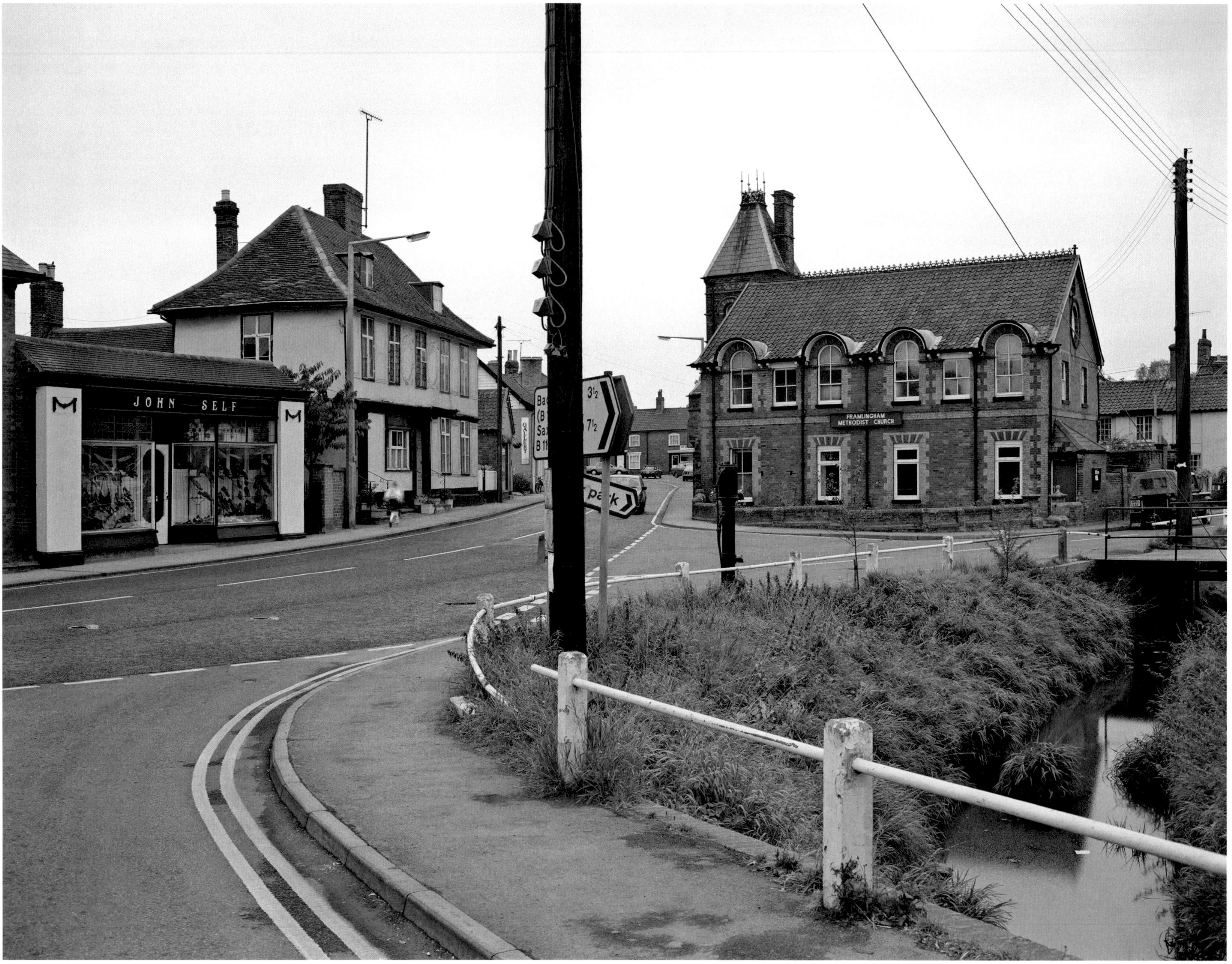

68   Framlingham, 1985

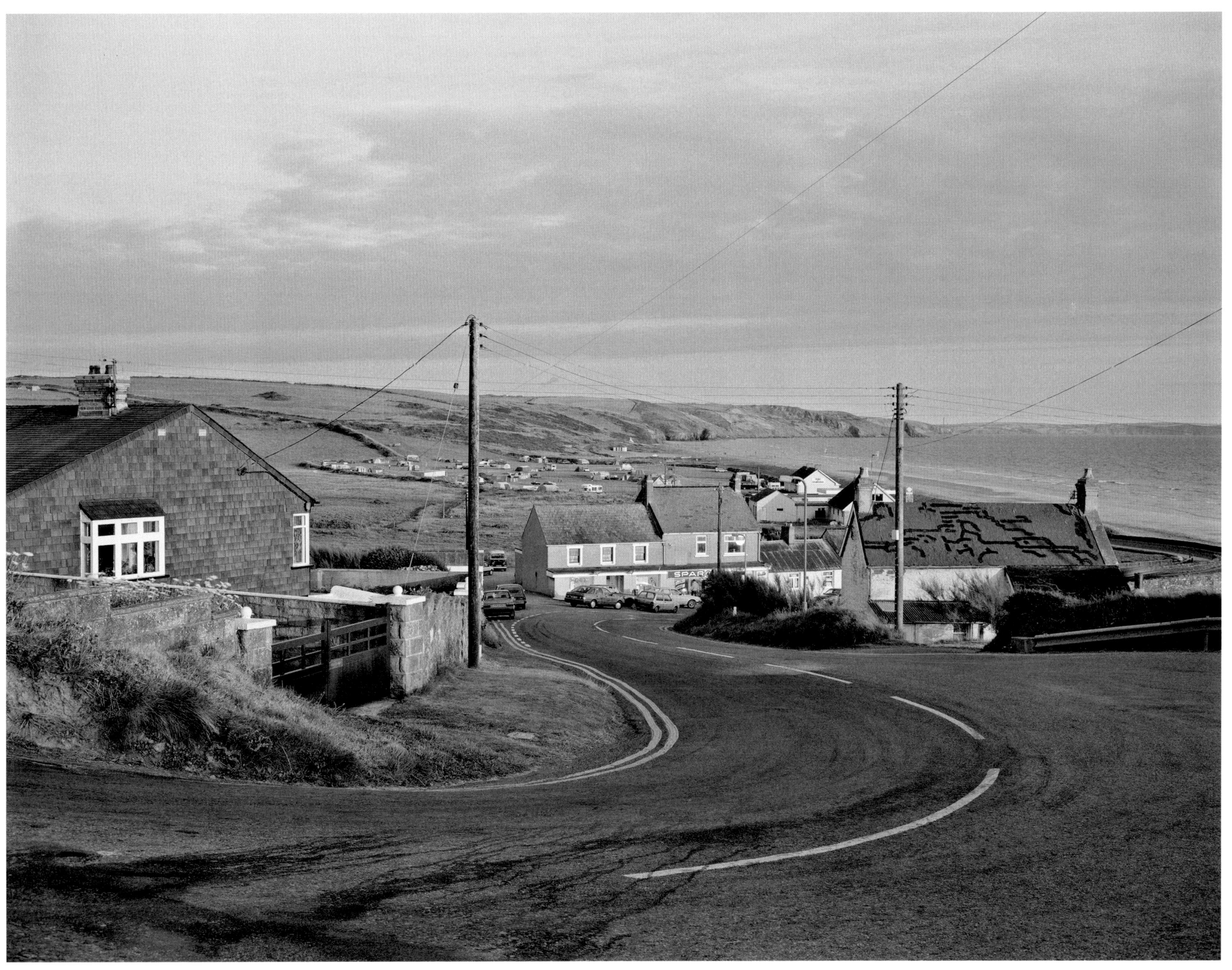

Newgale, 1988

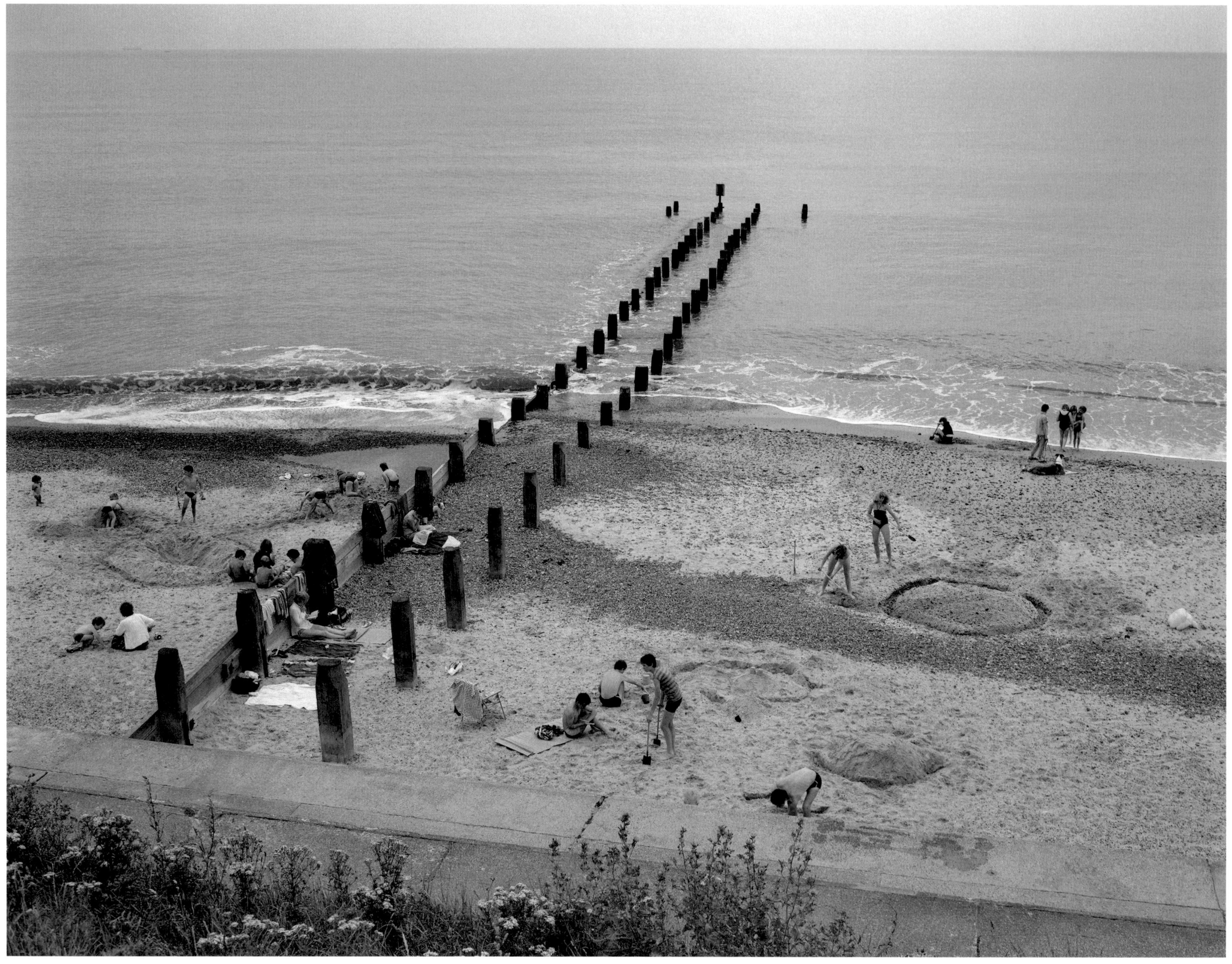

70   Southwold, 1985

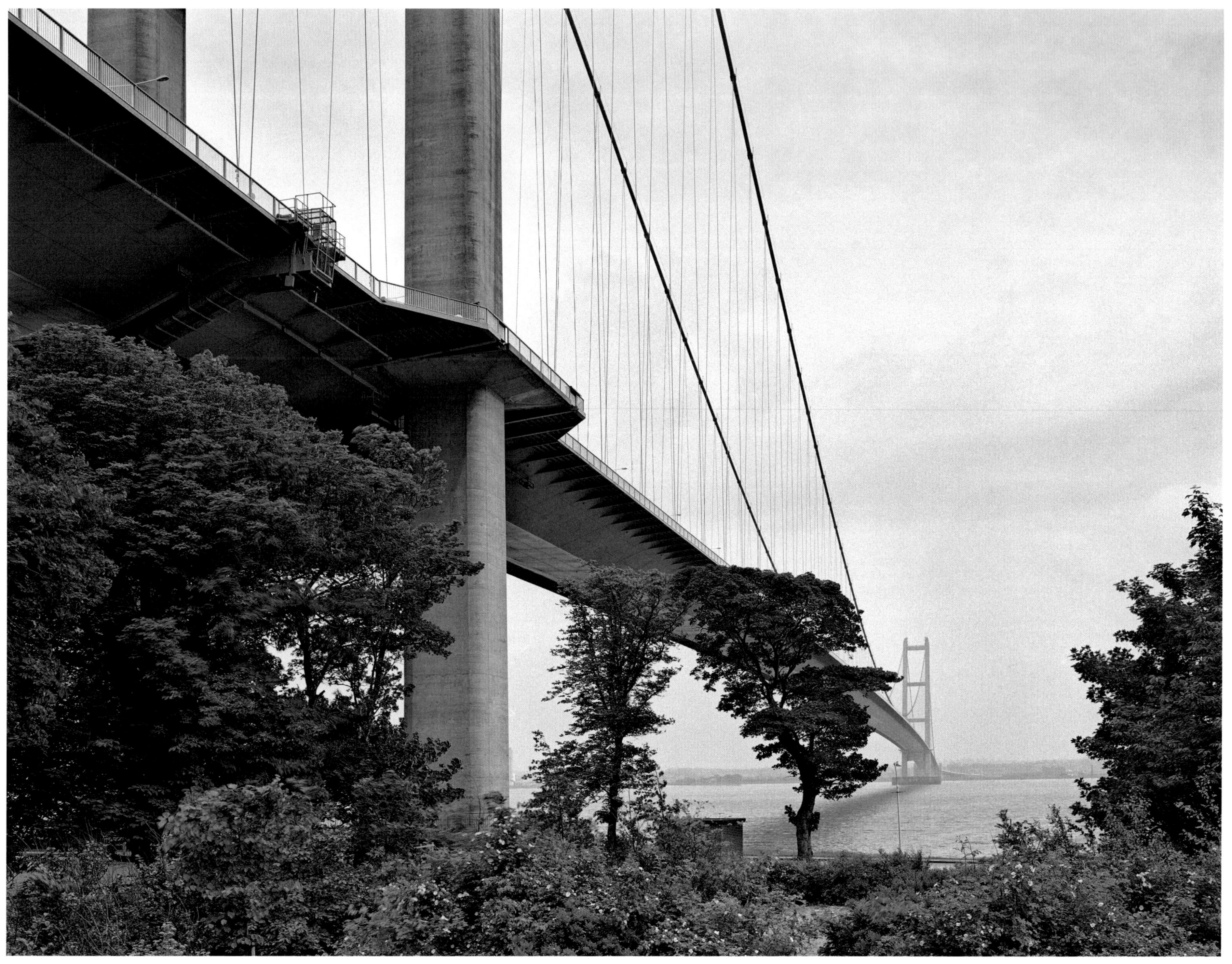

Humber Bridge, 1990

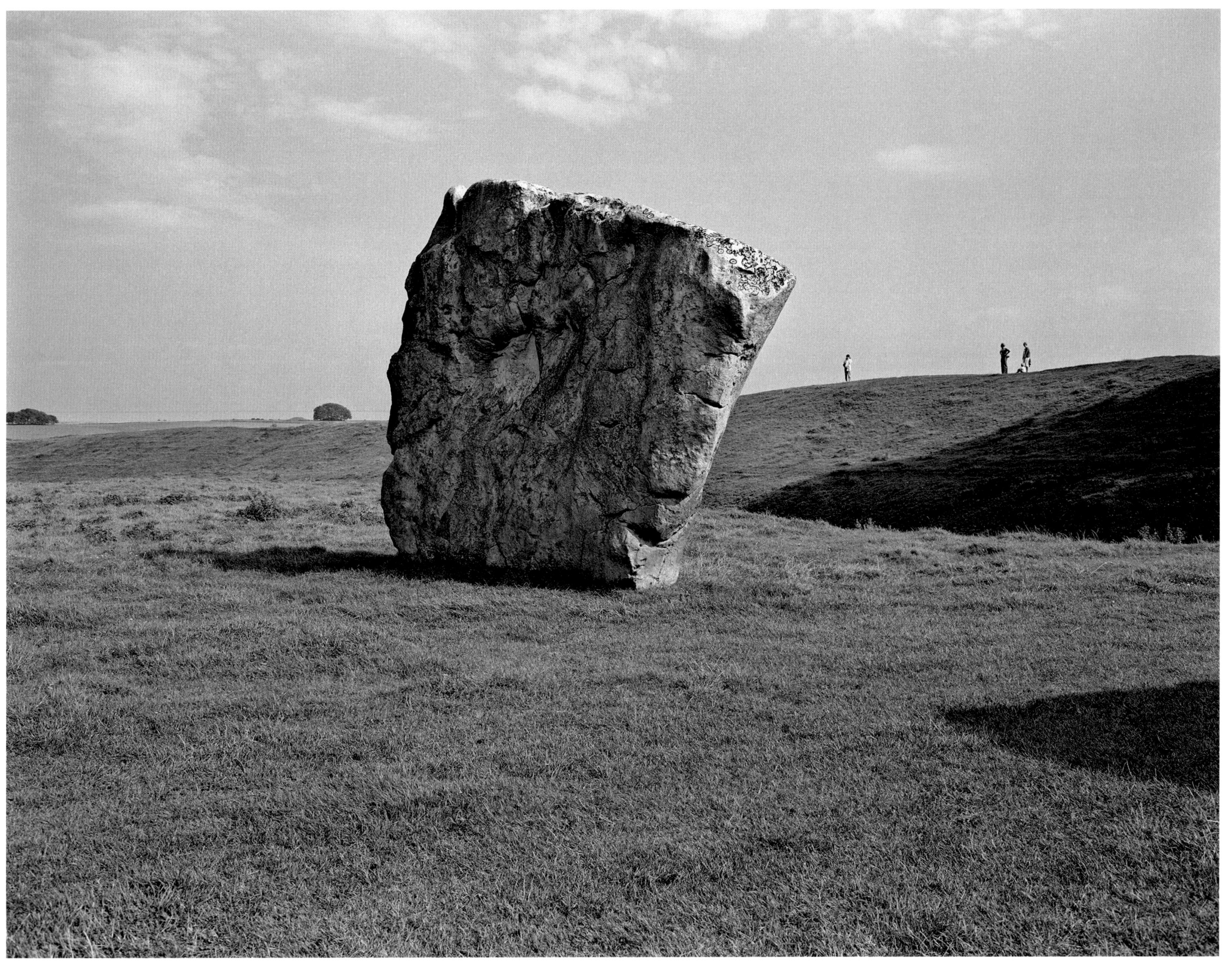

Avebury, 1985

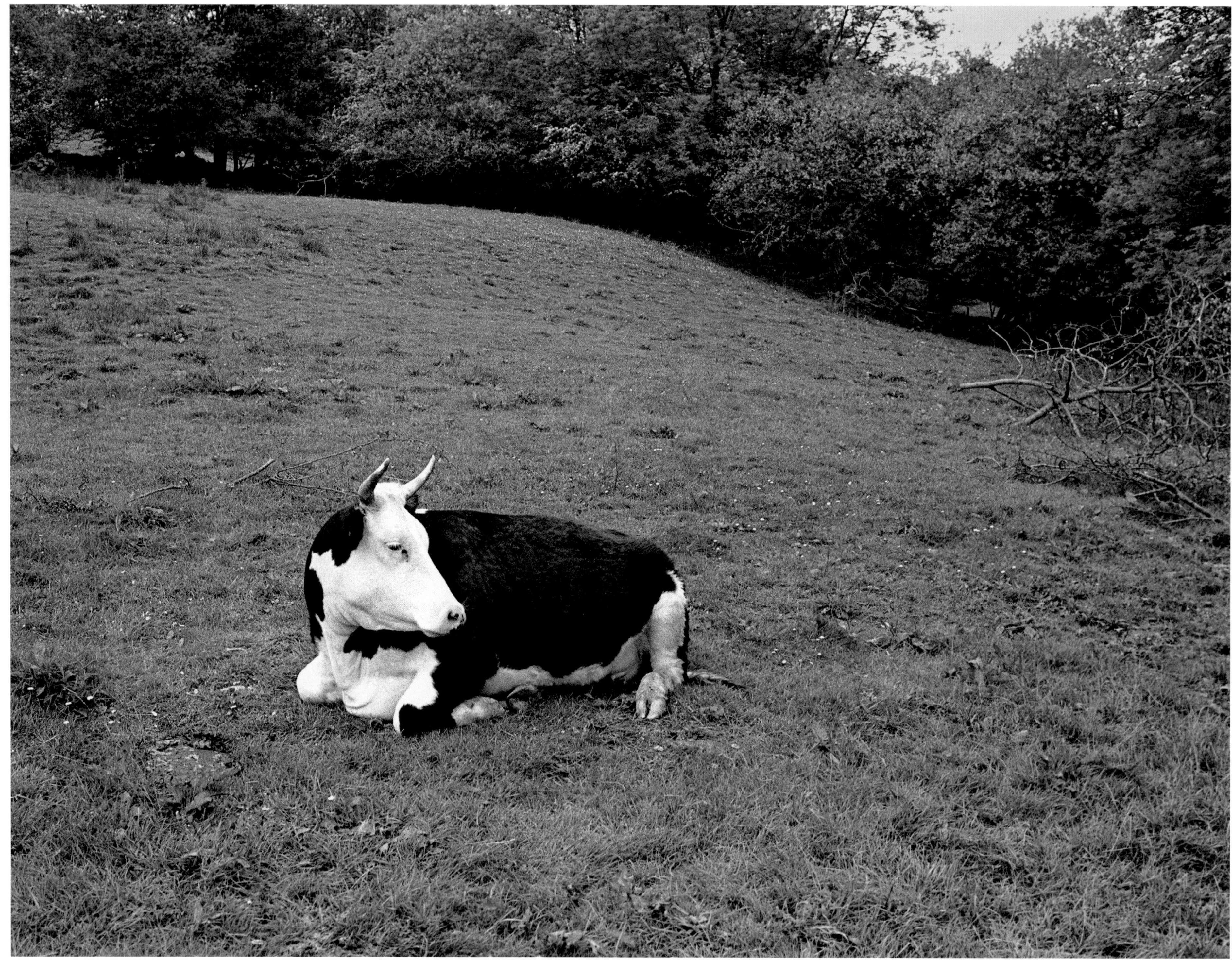

74   Wales, 1983

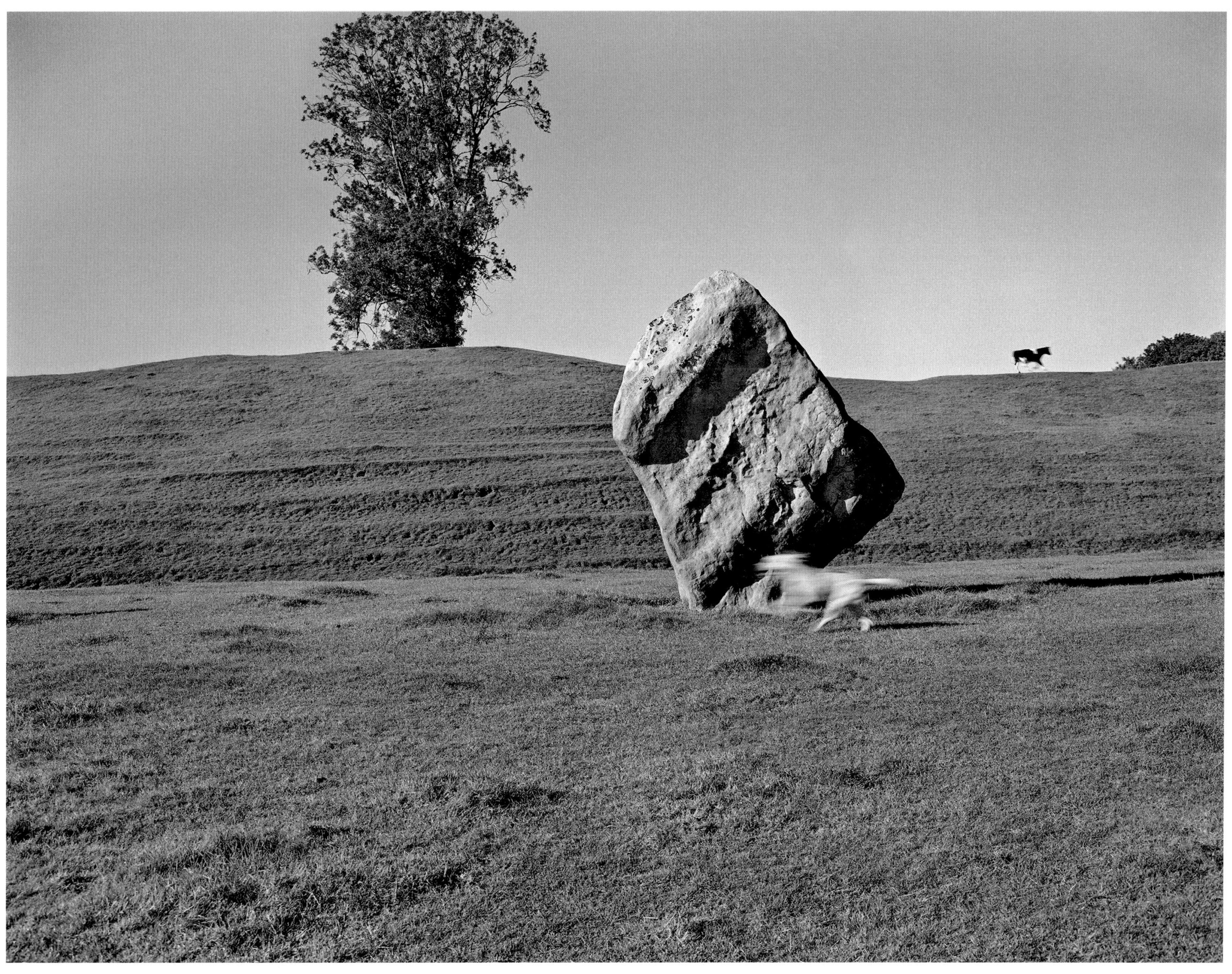

Avebury, 1985

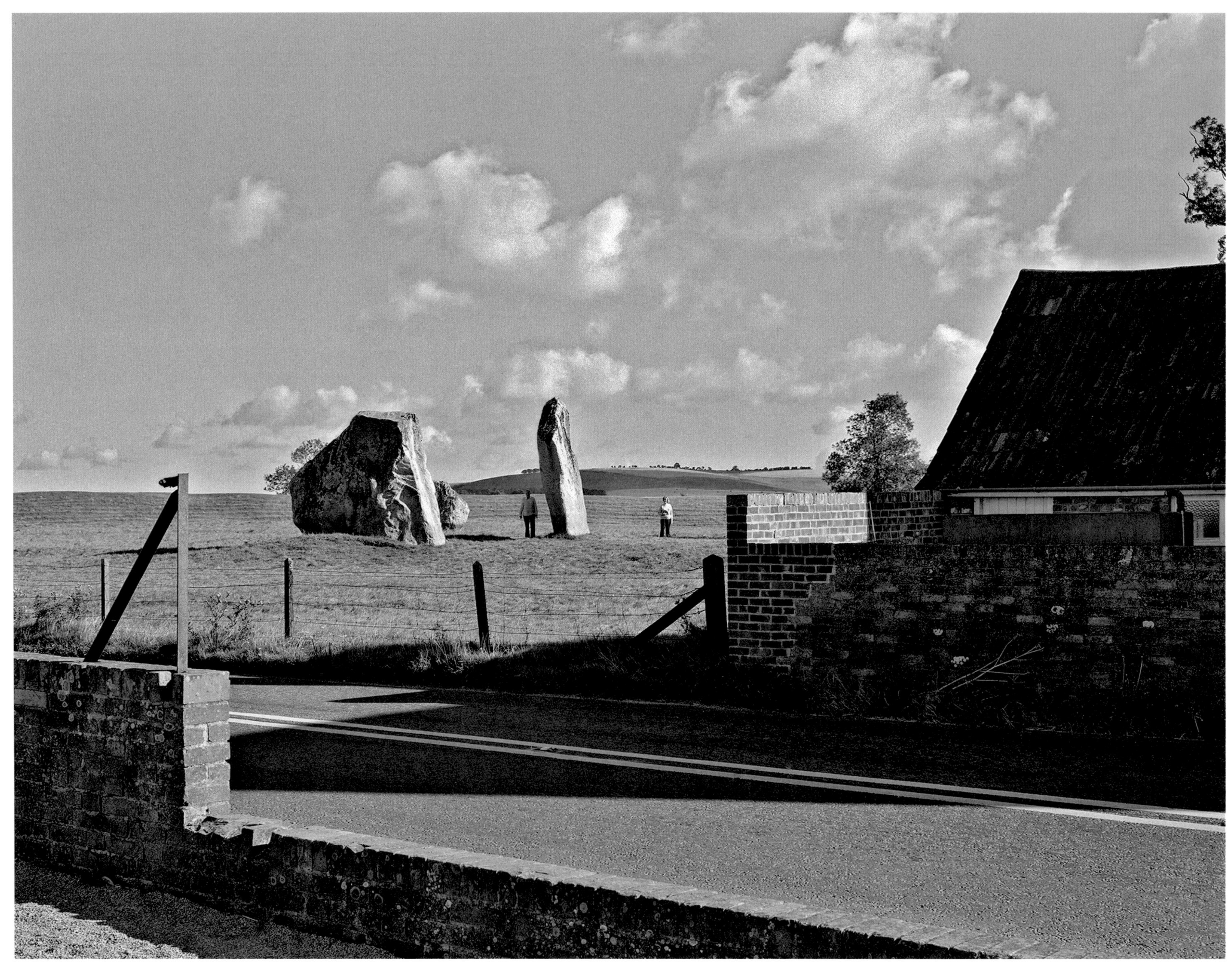

The Cove, Avebury, 1985

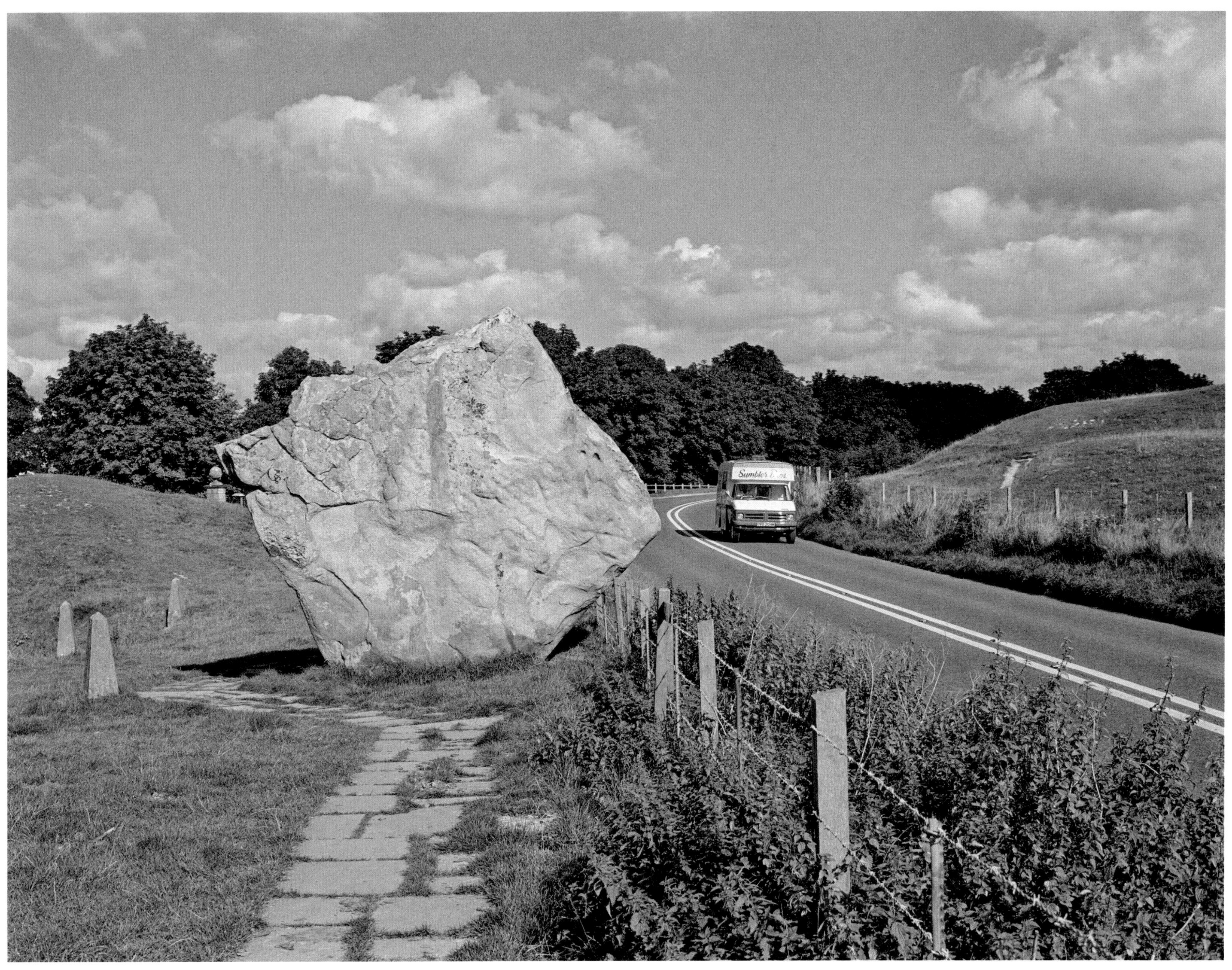

The Swindon Stone, Avebury, 1985   77

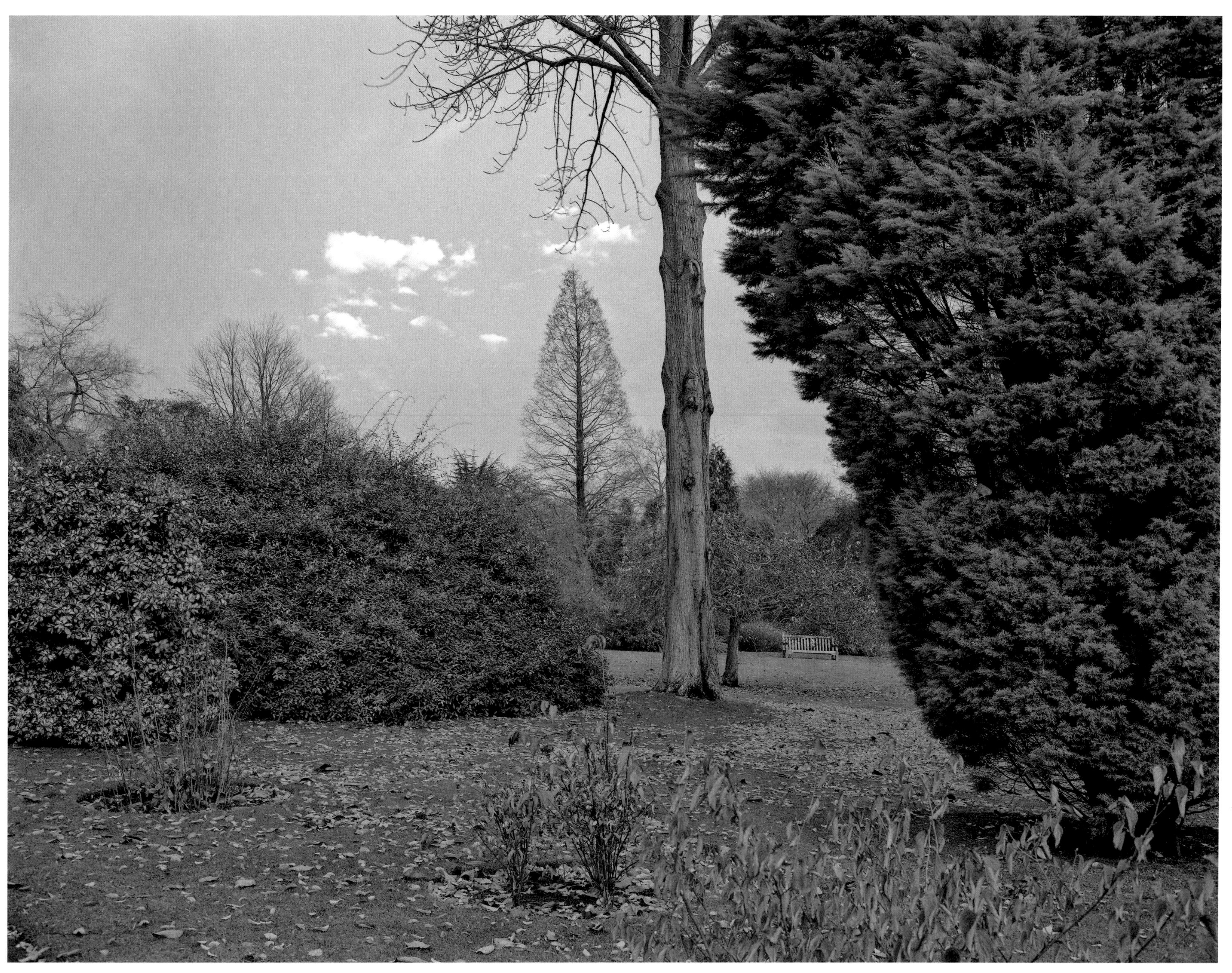

Bath Botanical Gardens, 1985

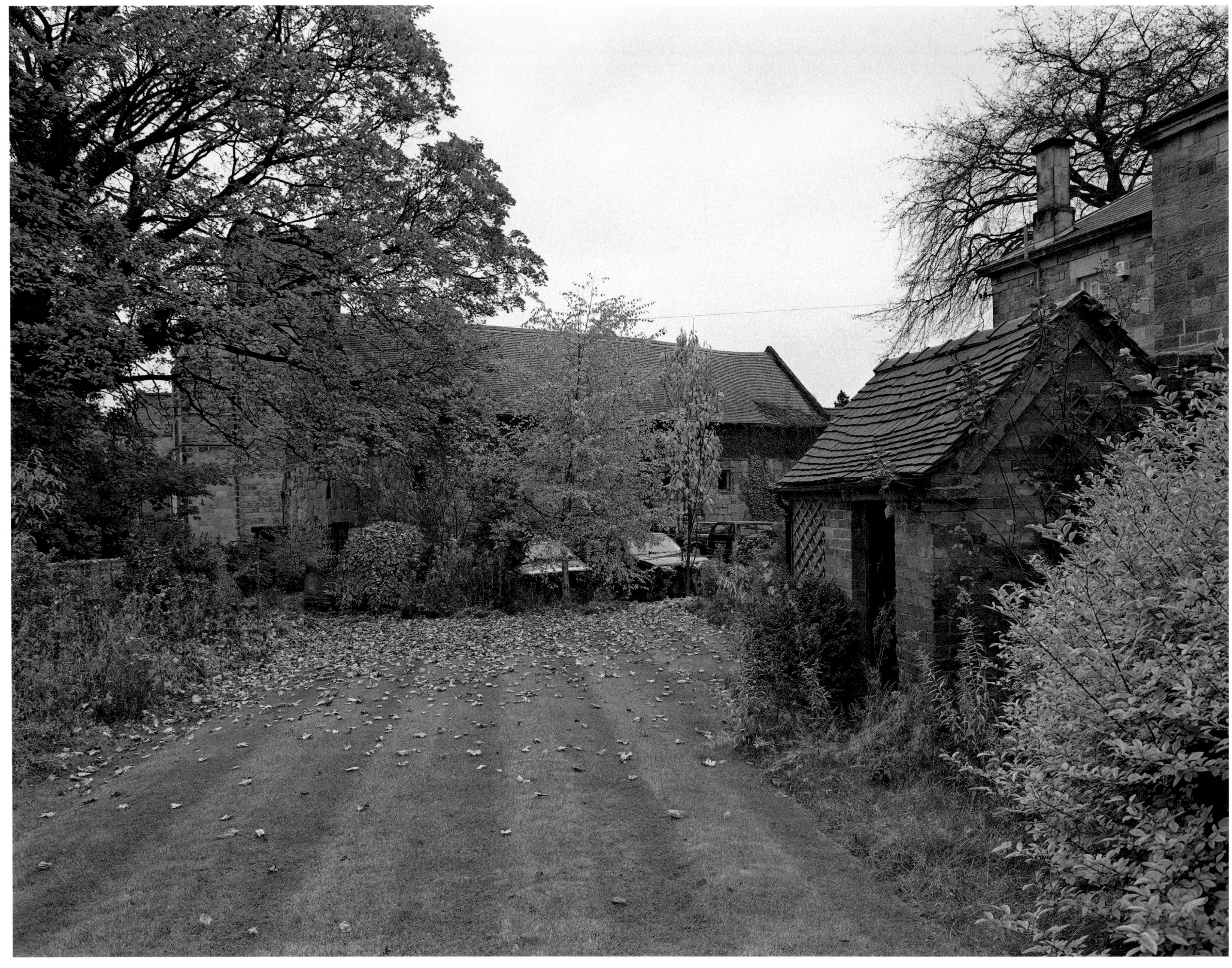

80   Melbourne, 1993

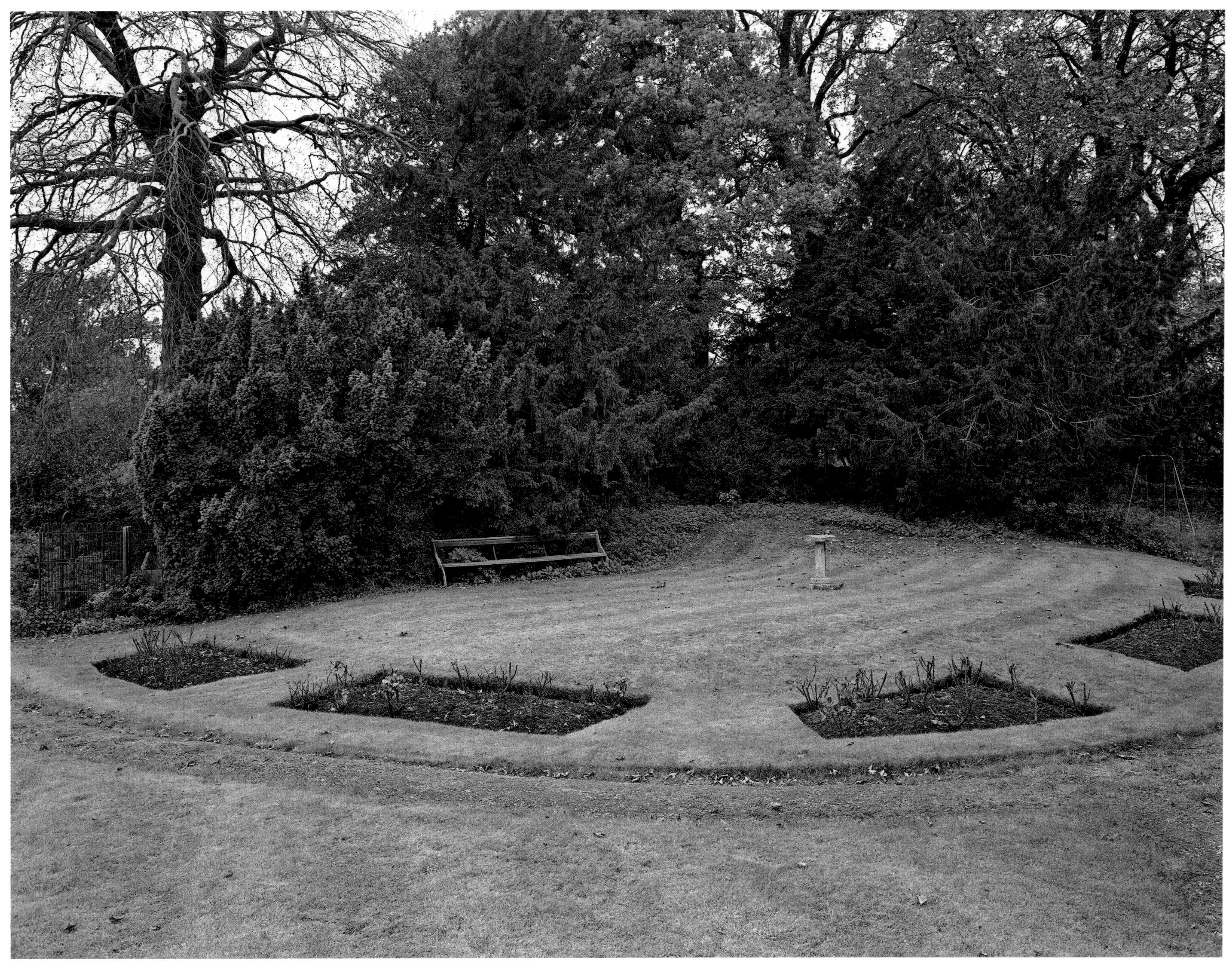

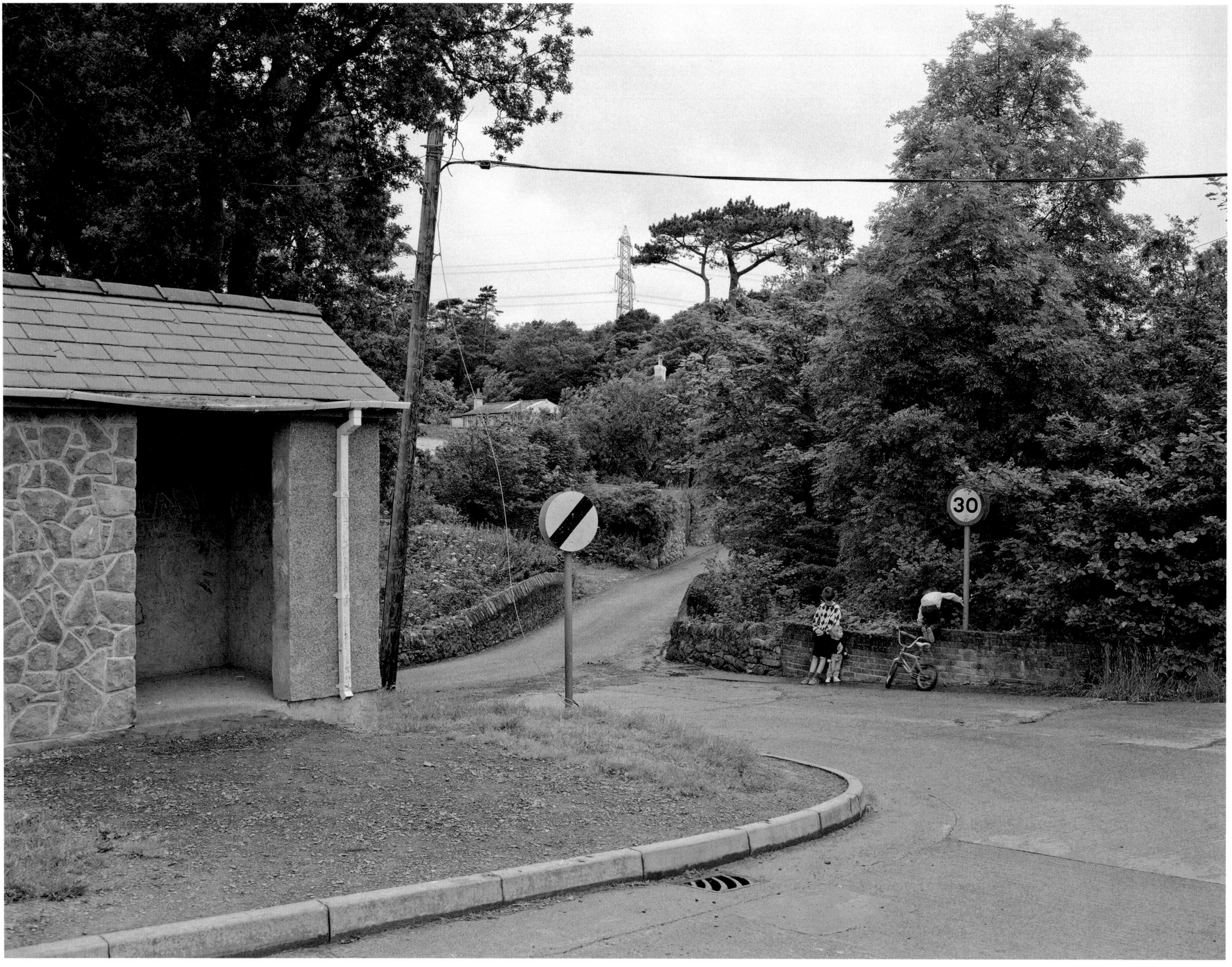

82   Wales, 1986

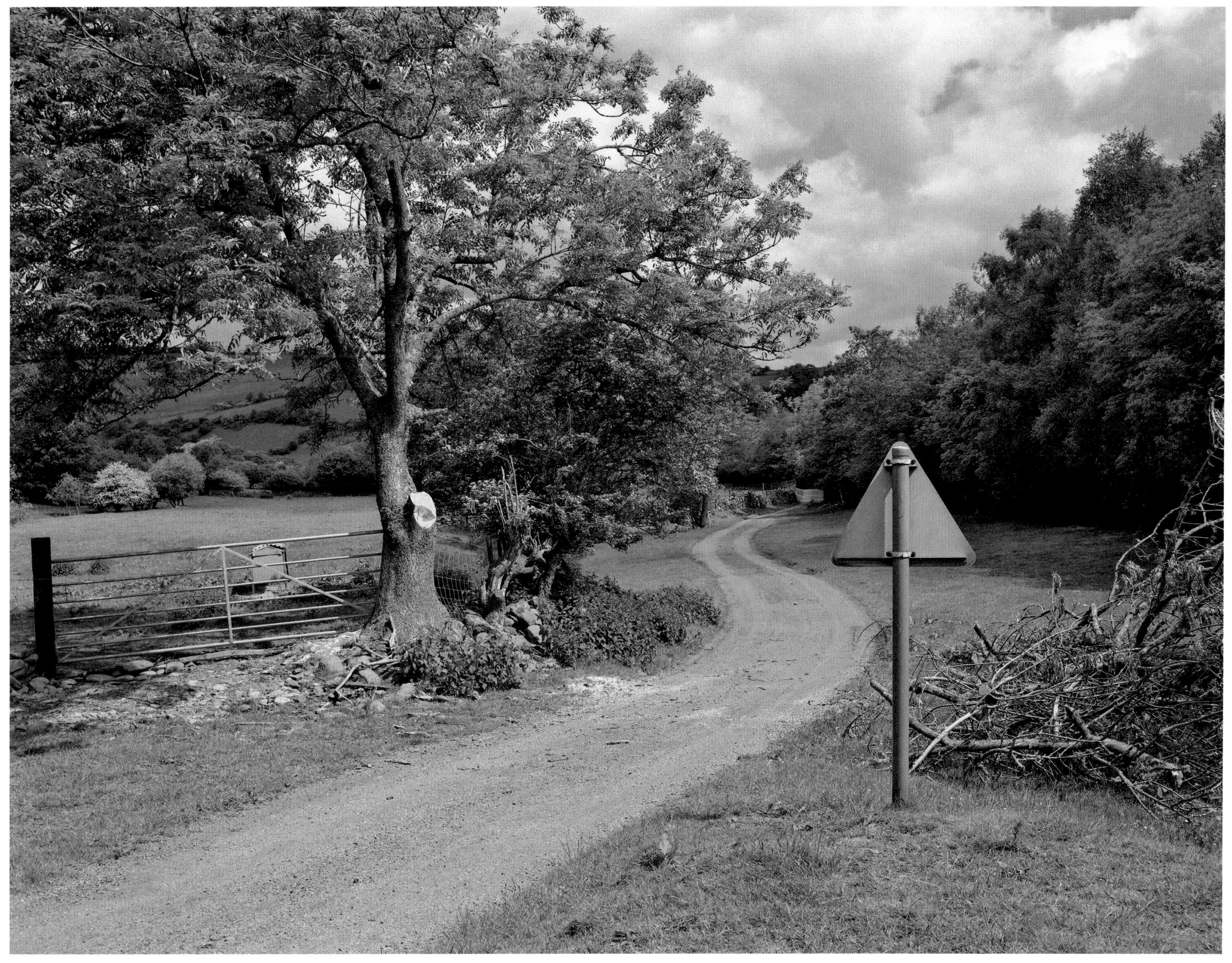

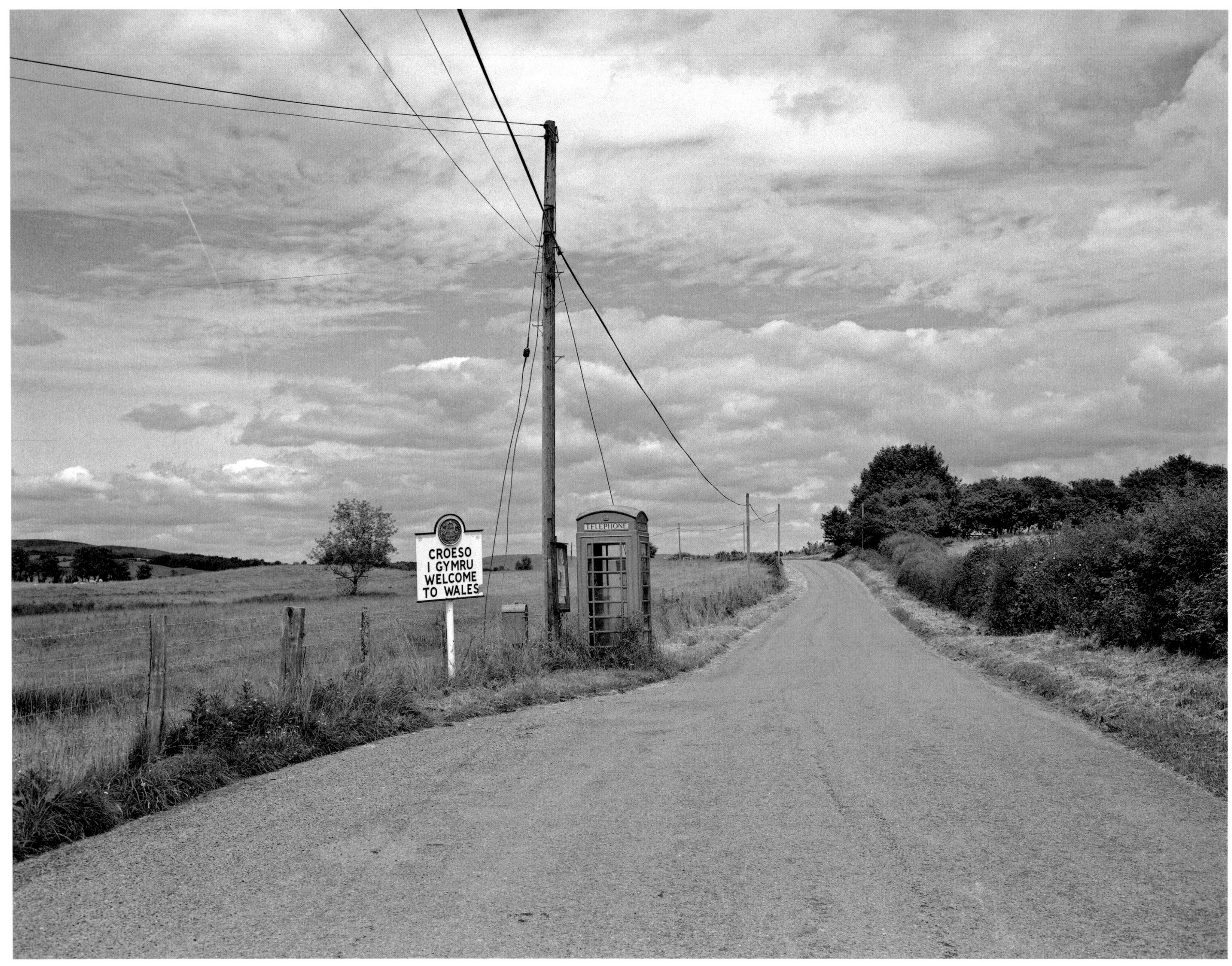

  Wales, 1987

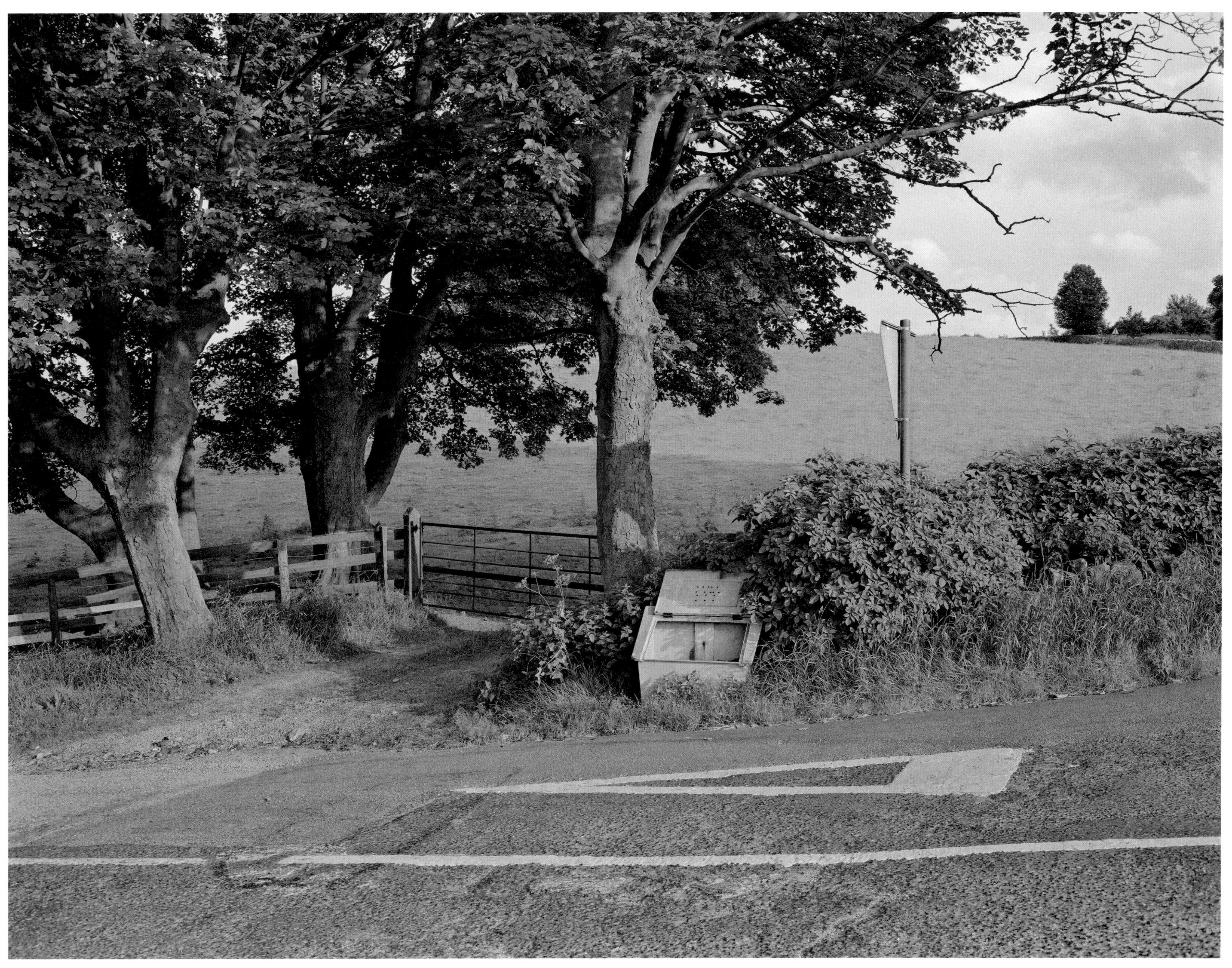

Derbyshire, 1986

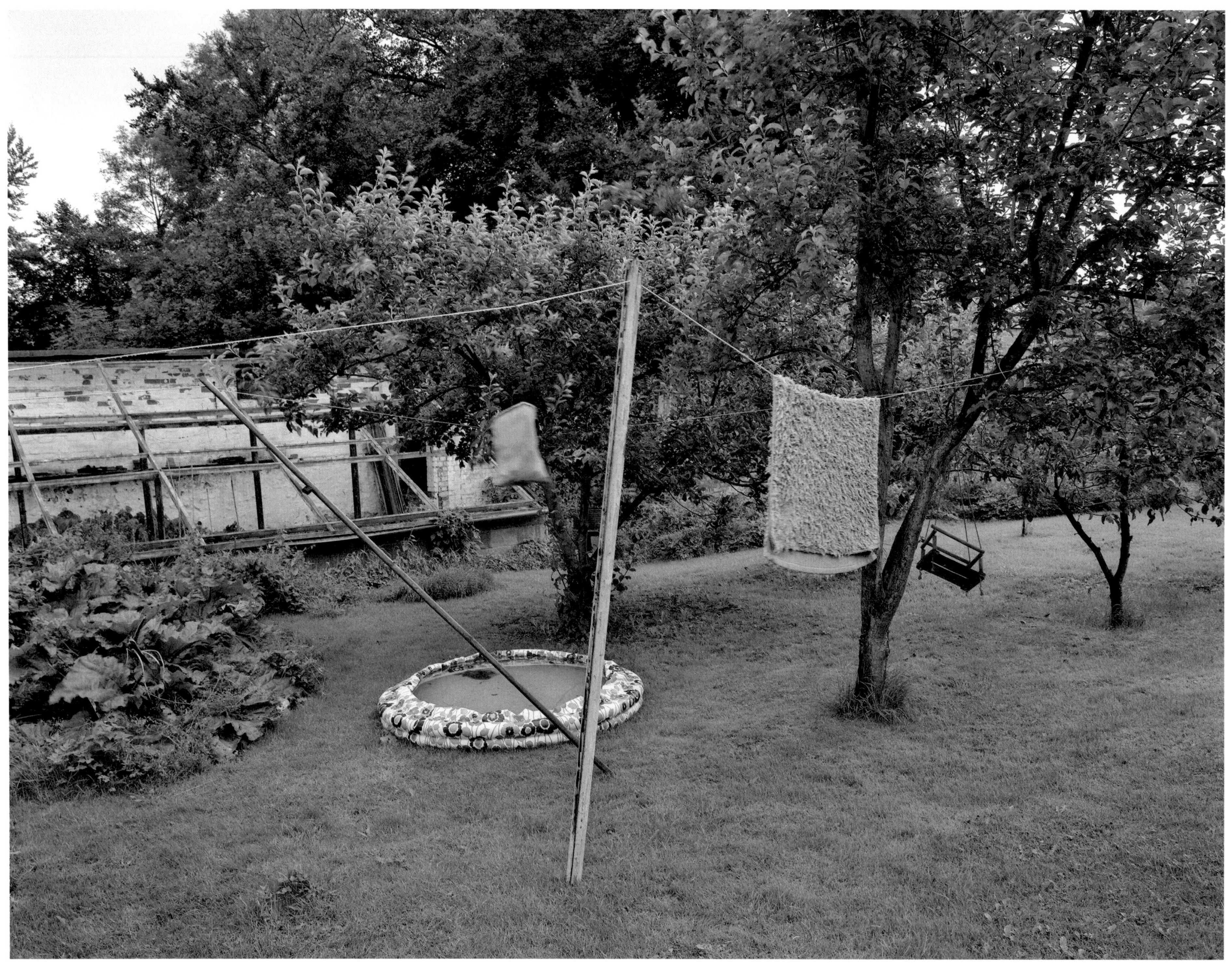

86   Norfolk, 1985

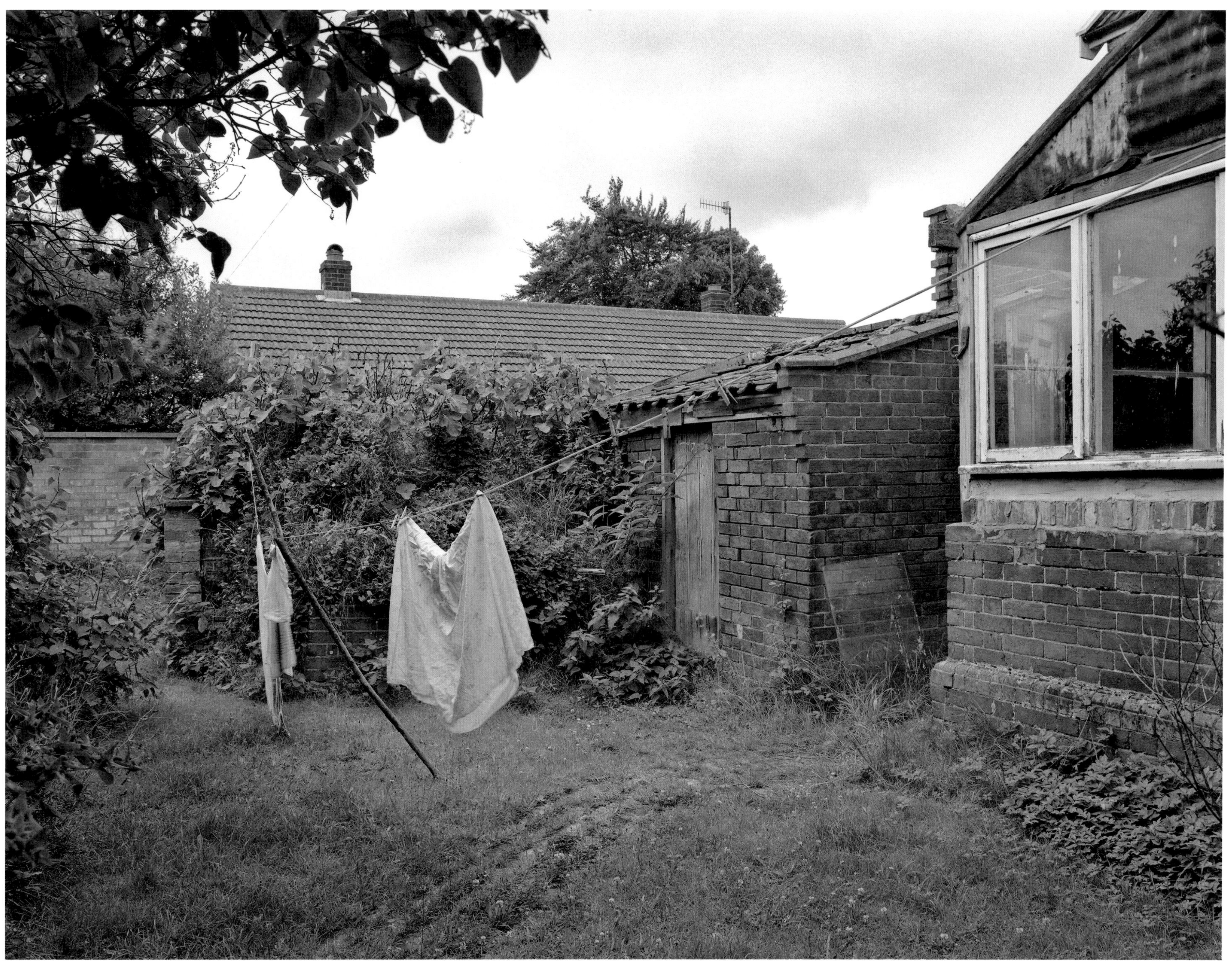

Norfolk, 1985

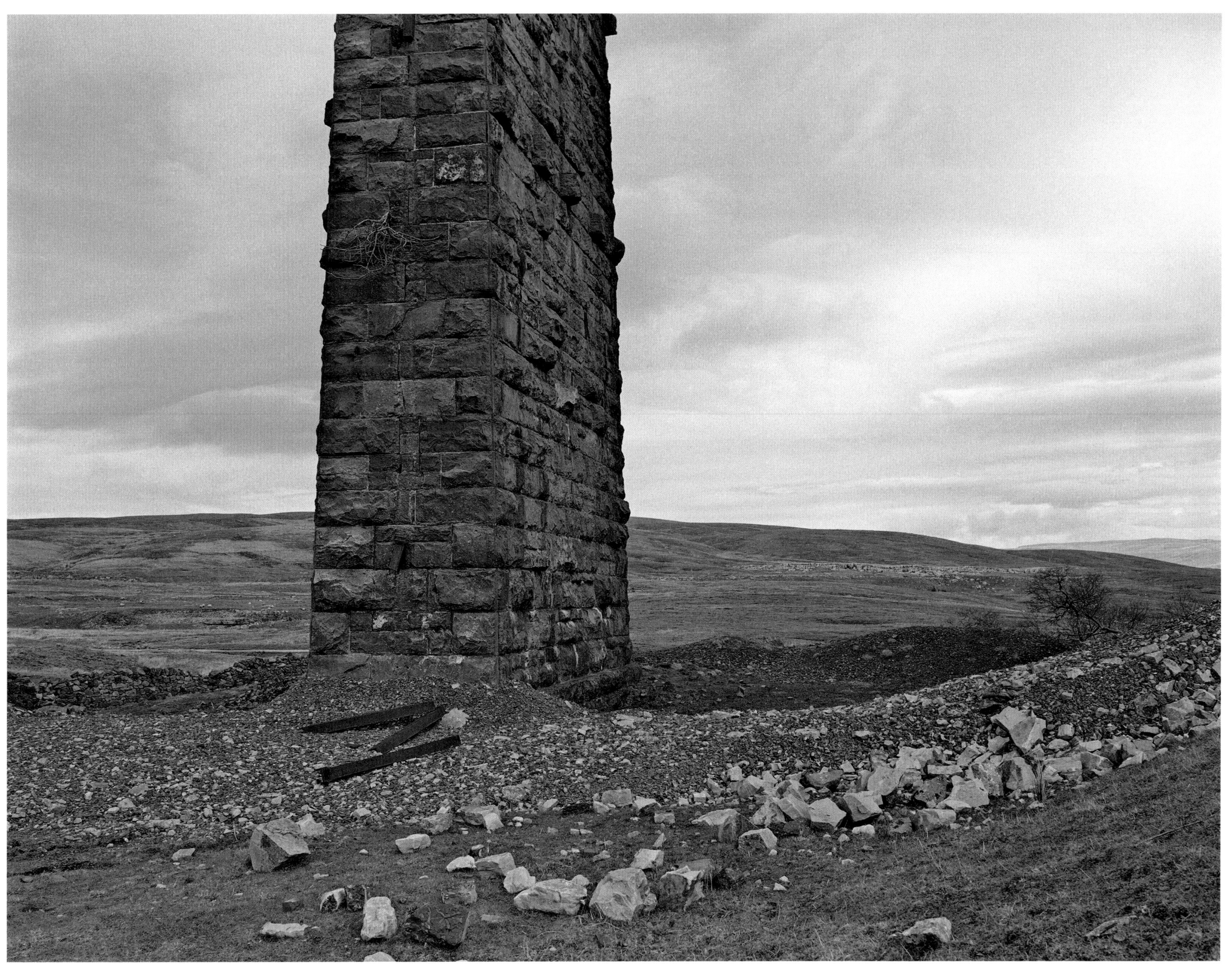

Ribblehead viaduct, 1990

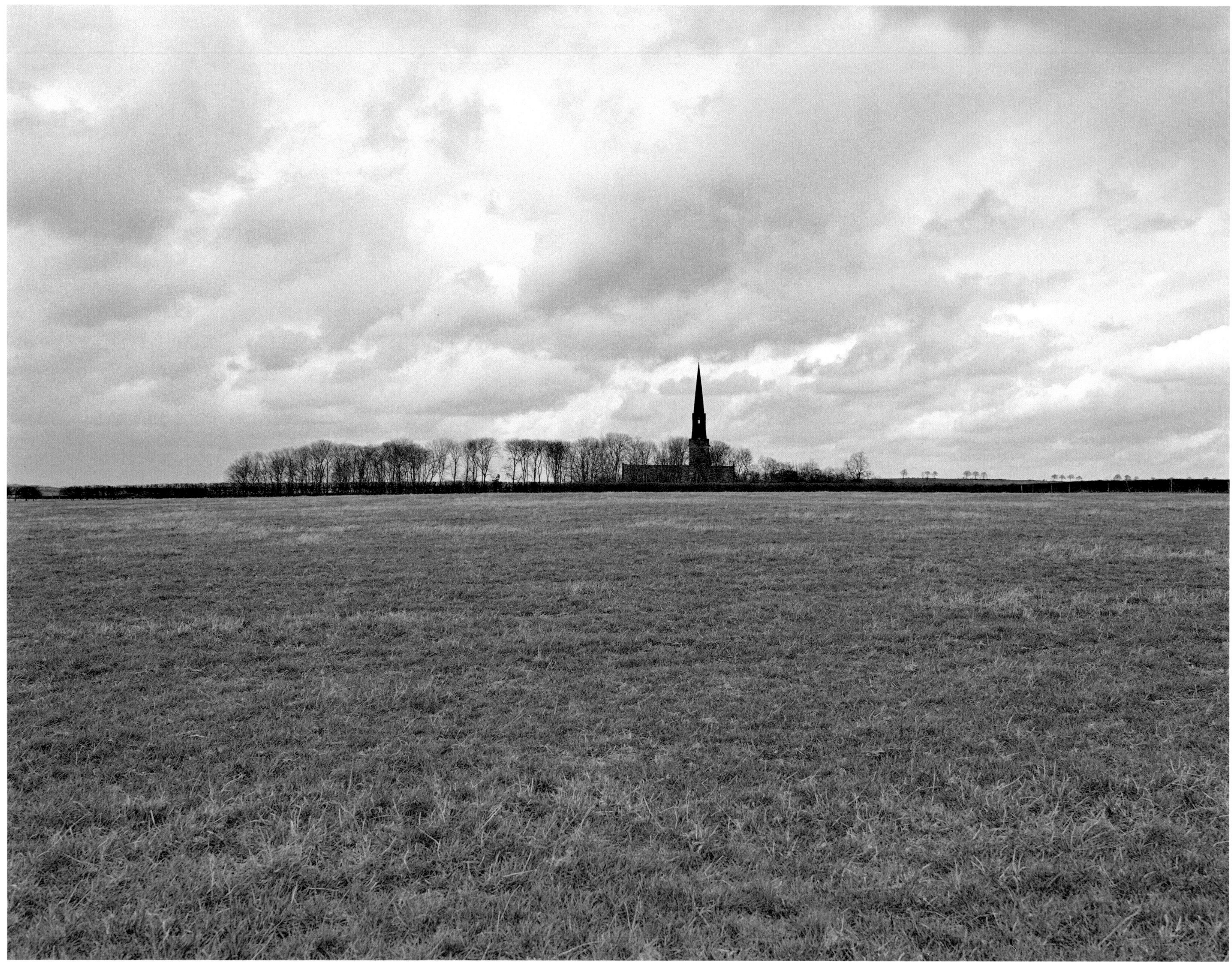

90   Wentworth, 1992

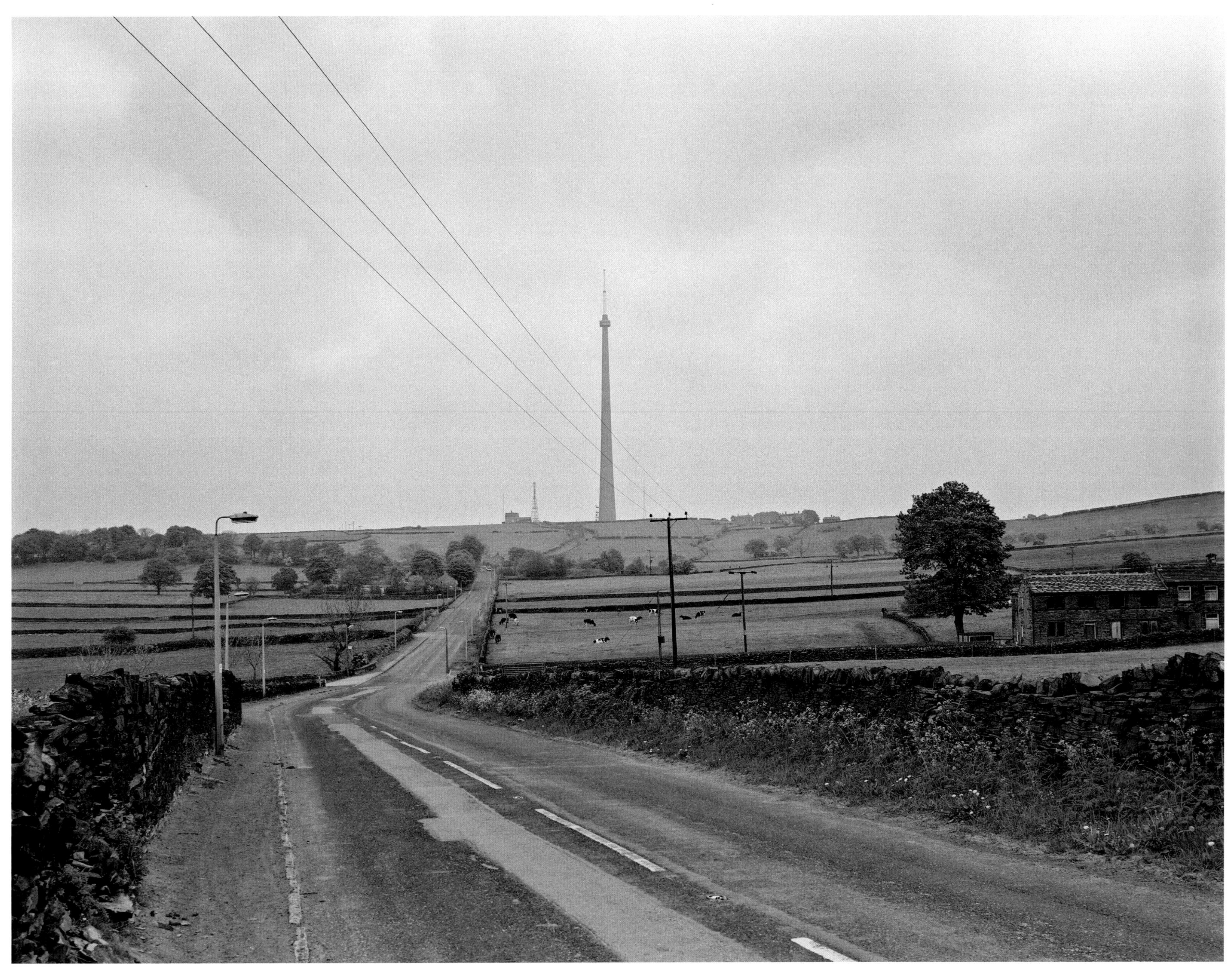

Emley Moor, 1990

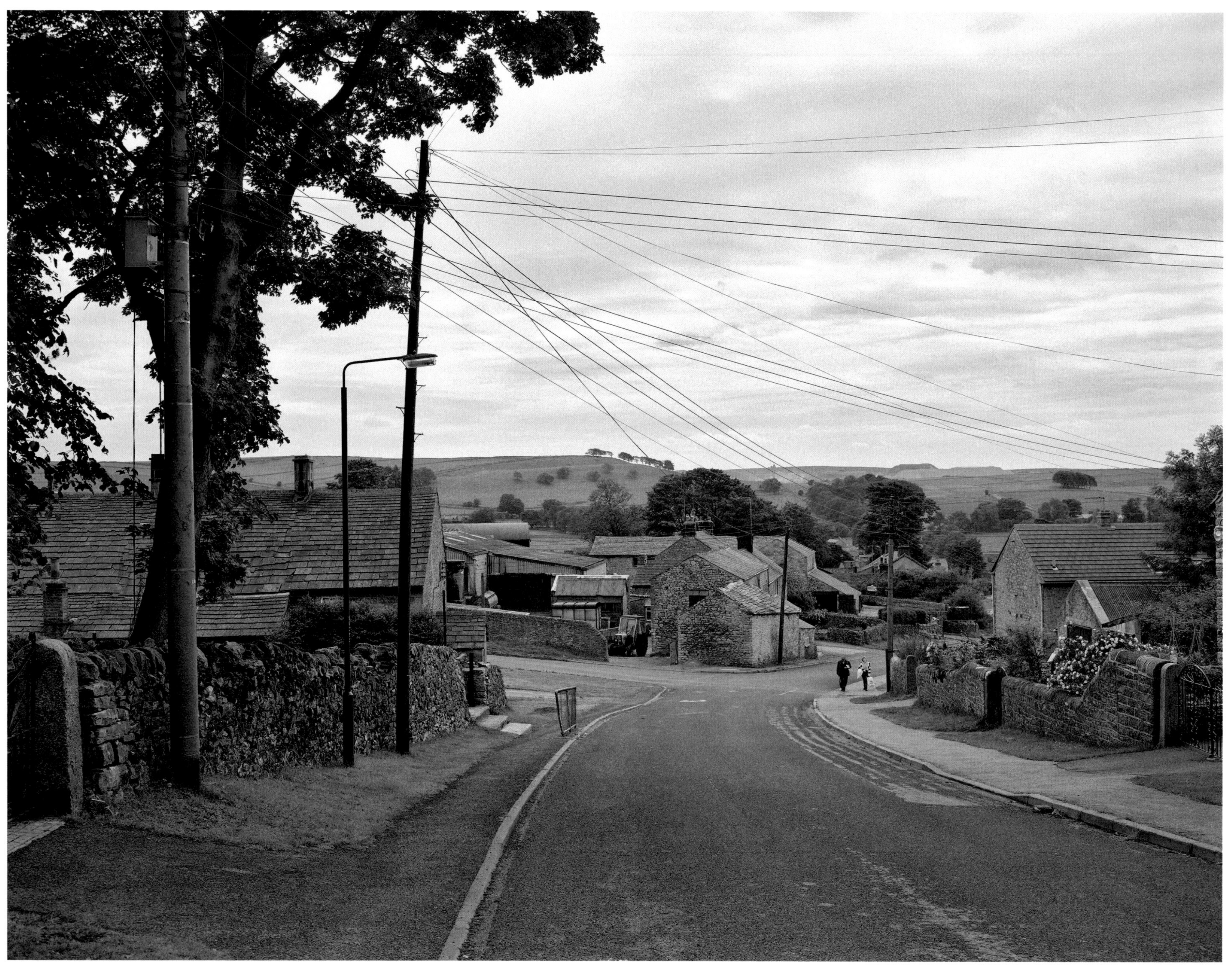

92   Derbyshire, 1986

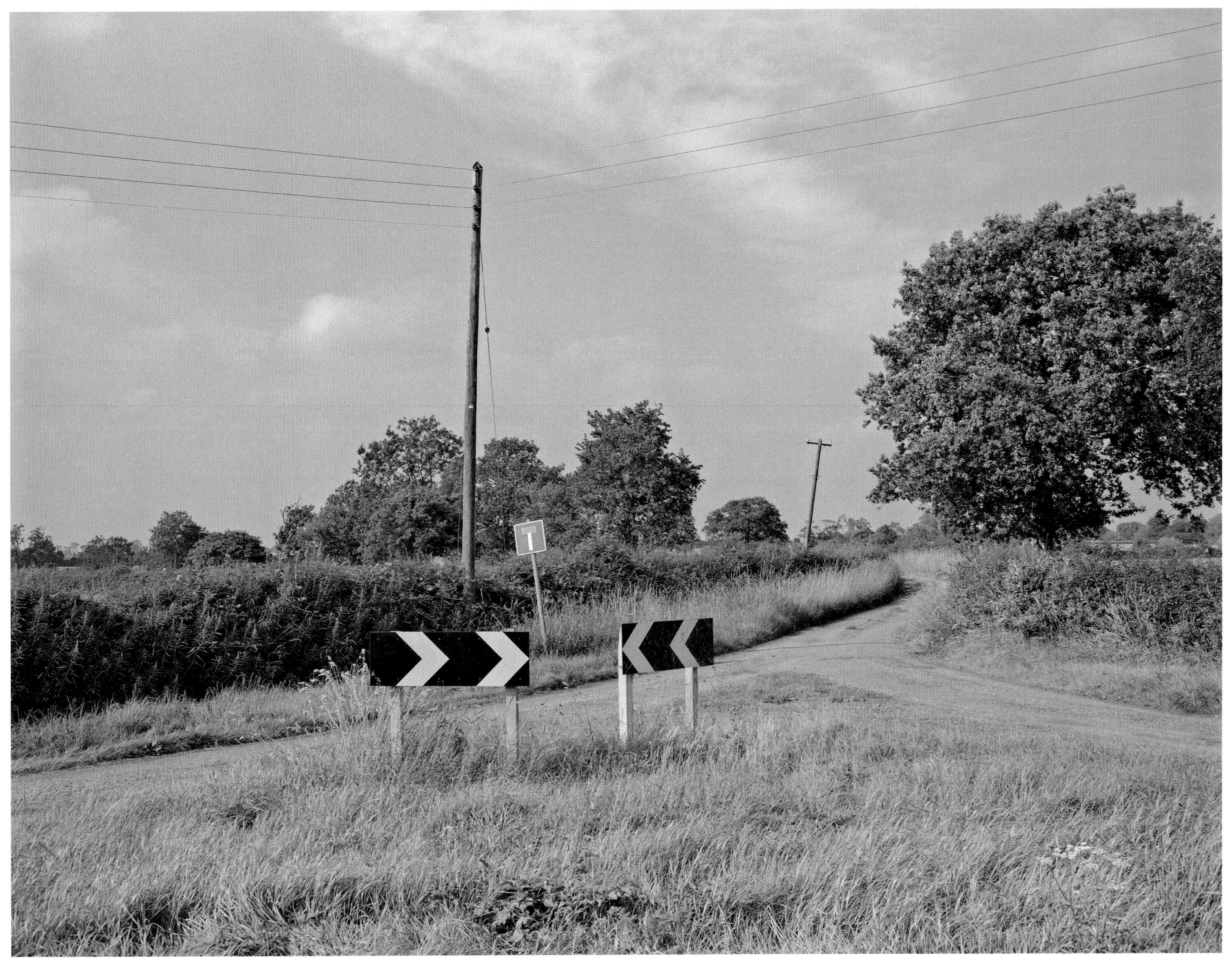

Derbyshire, 1986

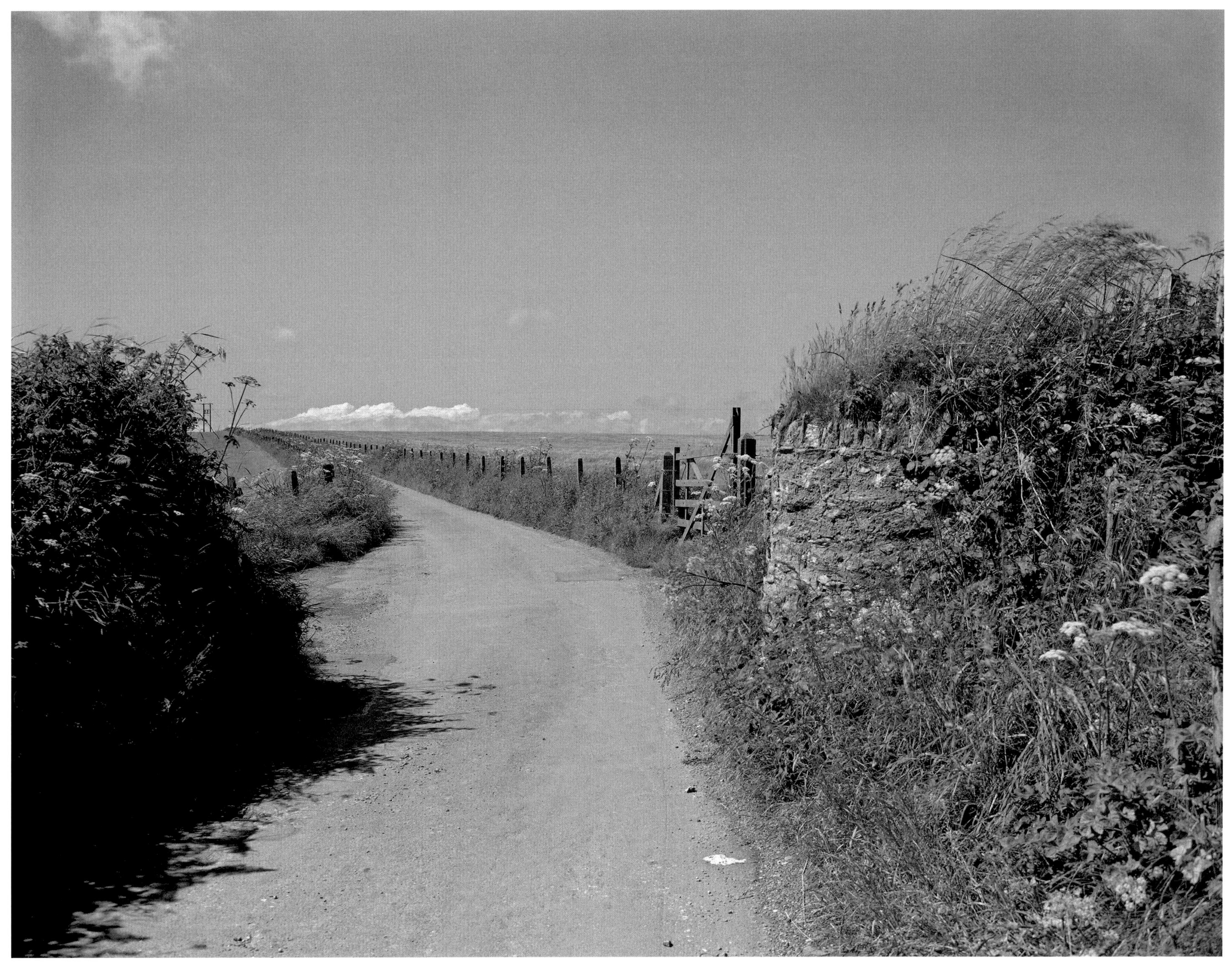

Devon, 1989

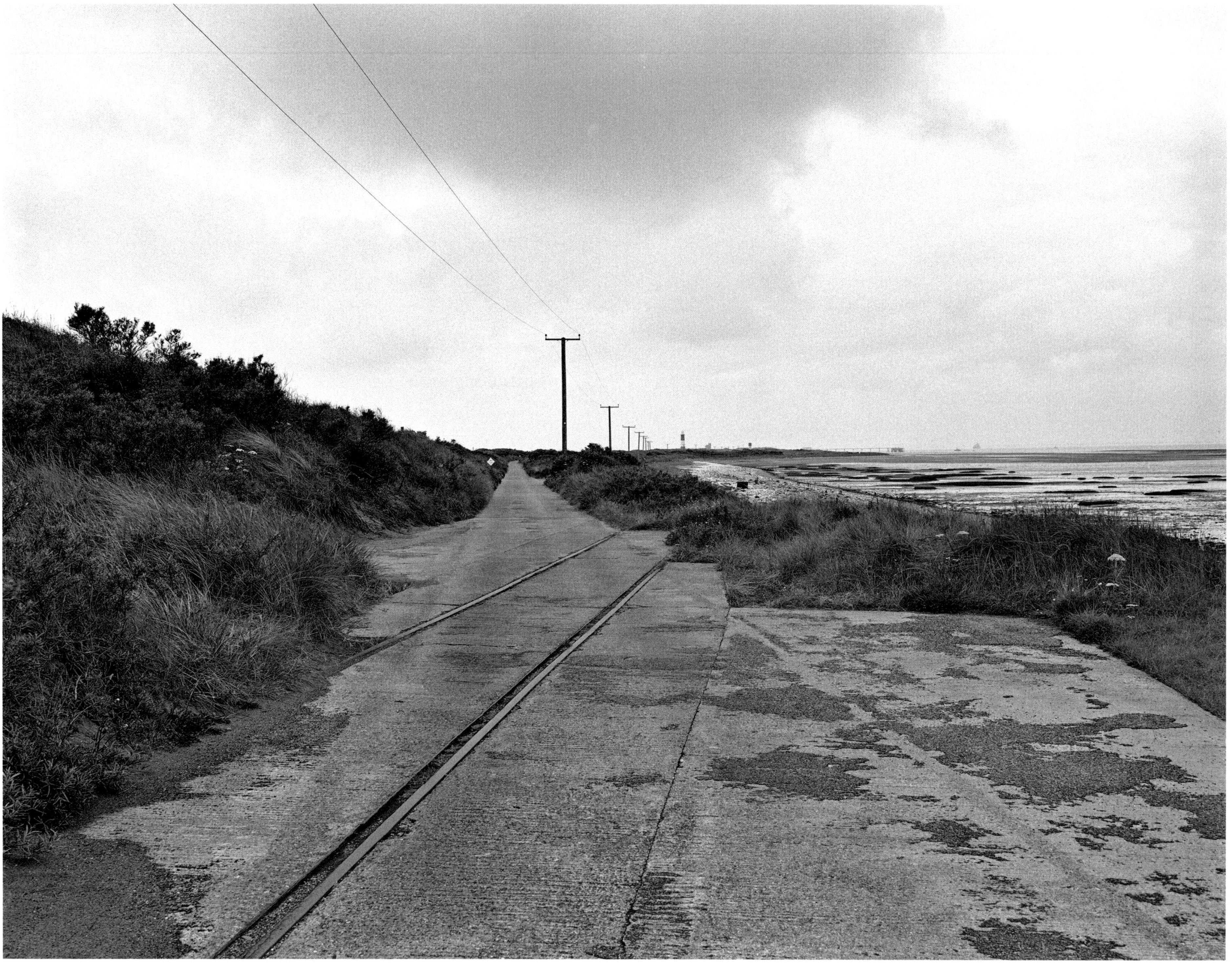

96   Spurn, 1990

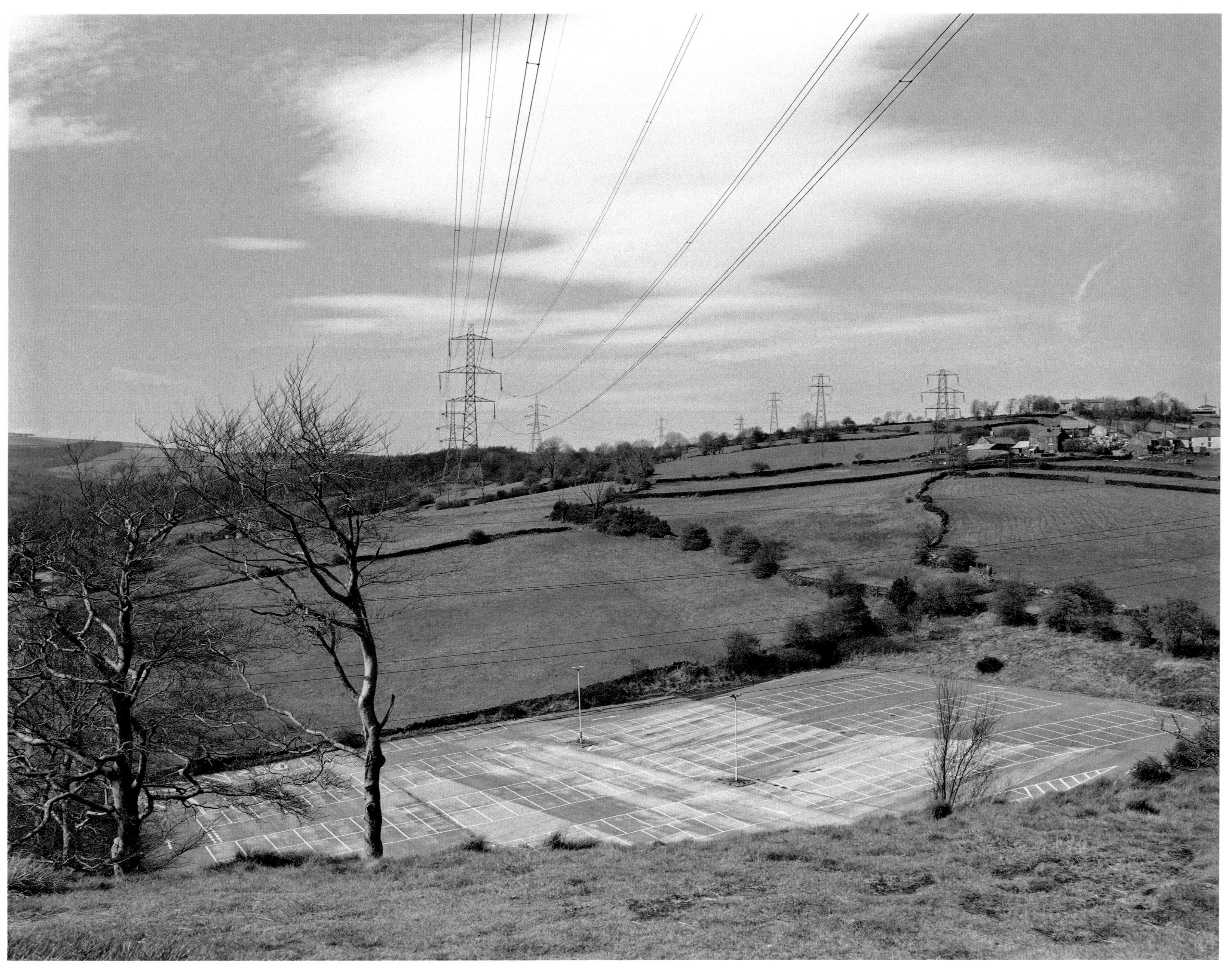

Middlewood, 1989

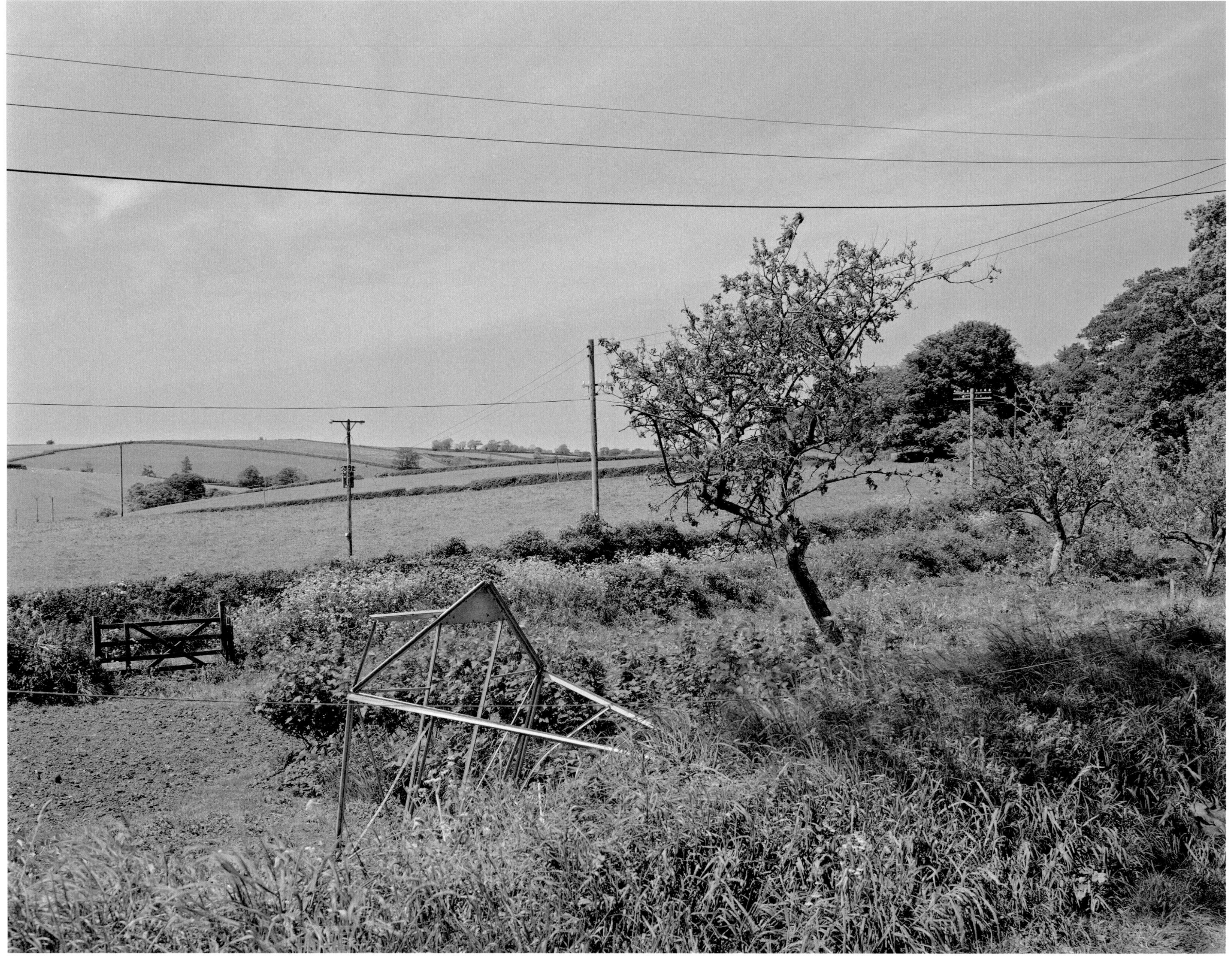

    Devon, 1989

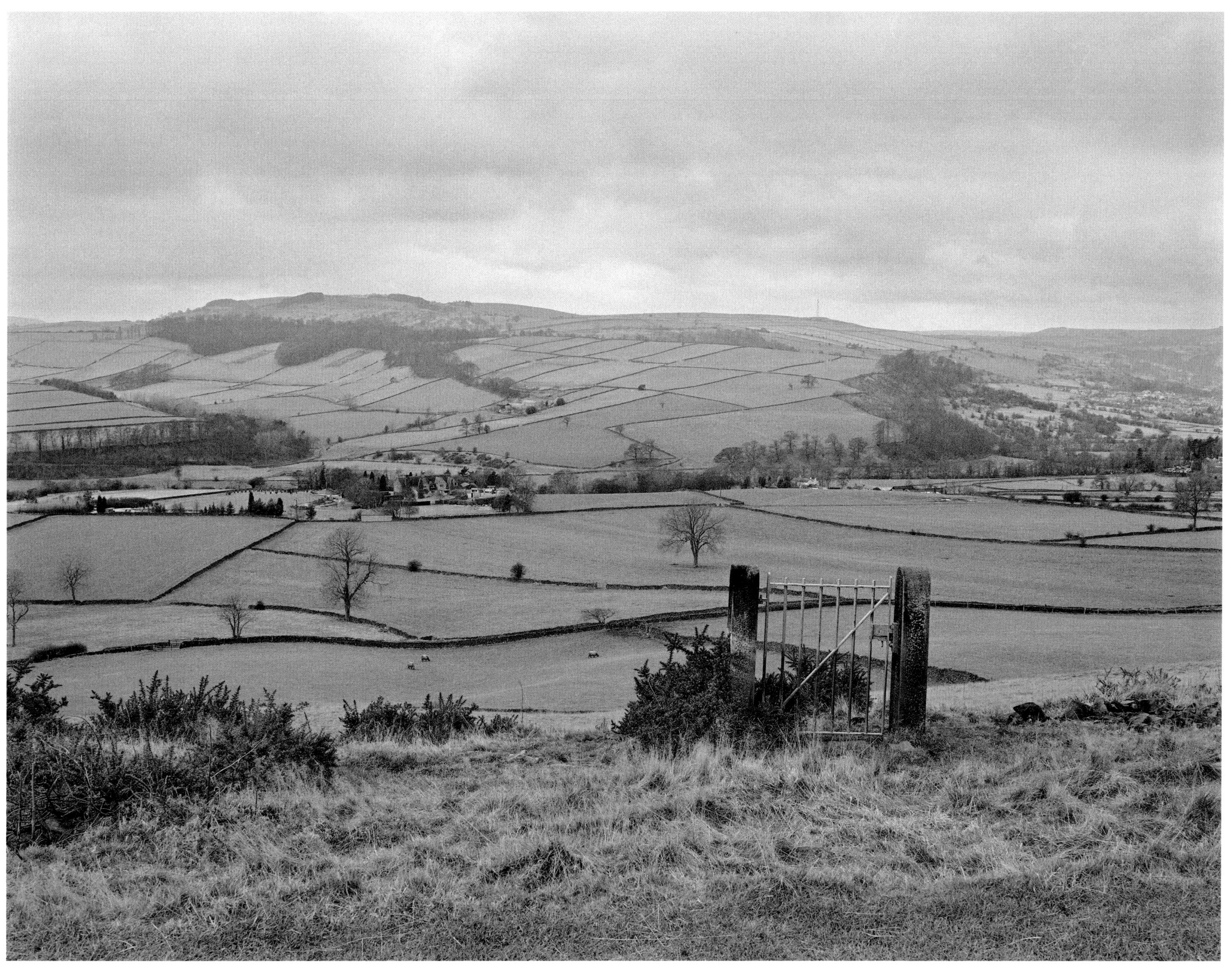

Derbyshire, 1993

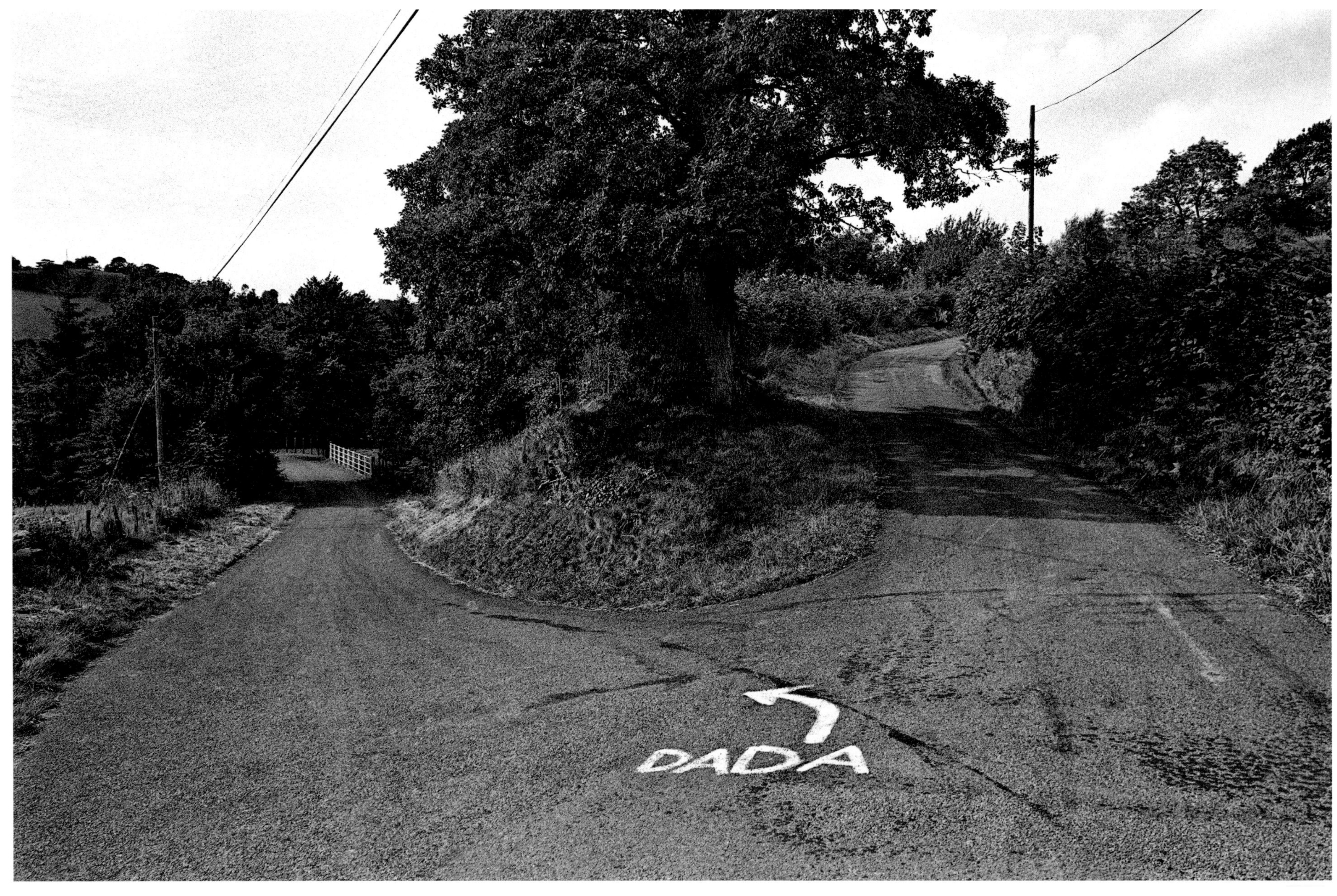

Wales, 1979

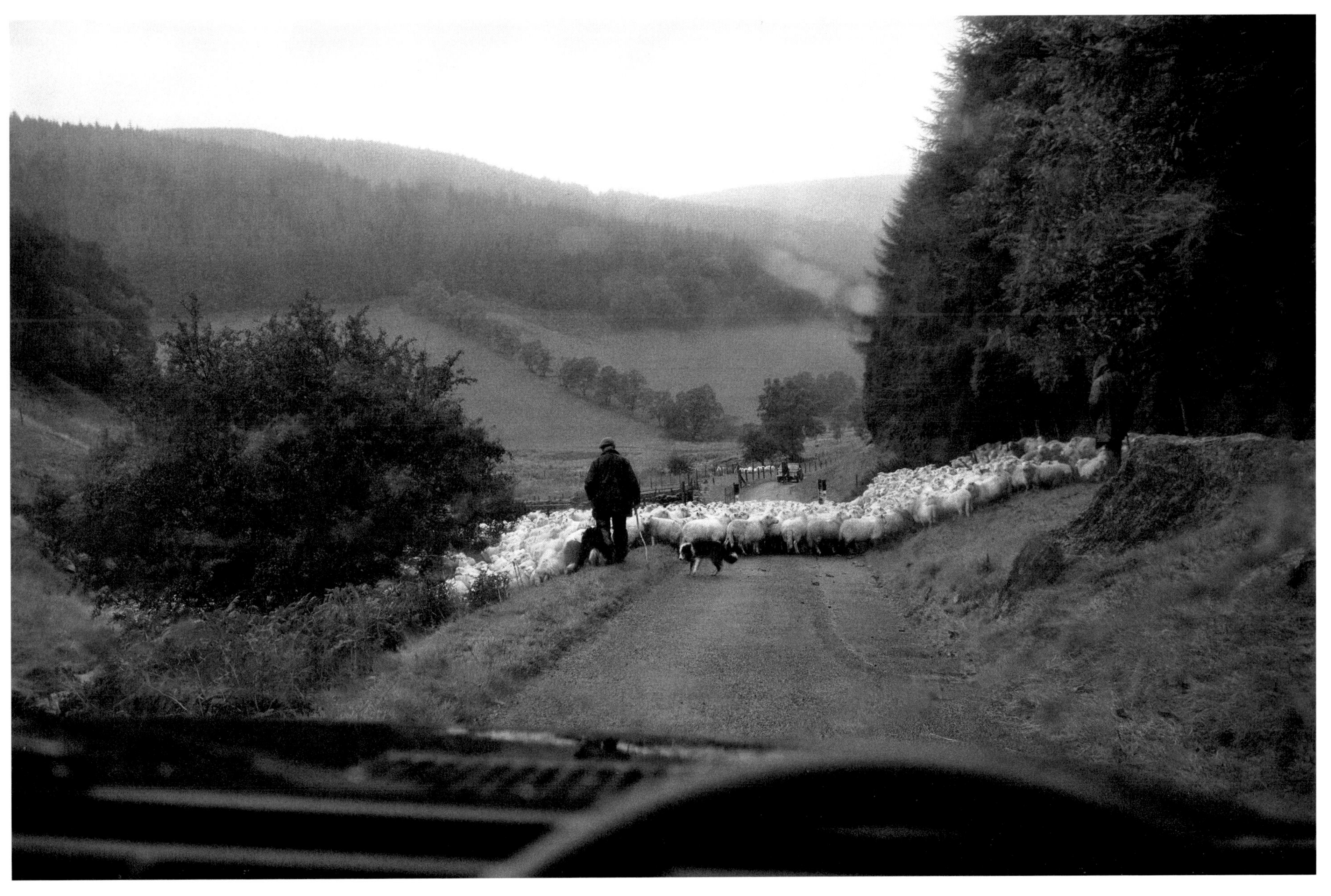

Wales, 1982

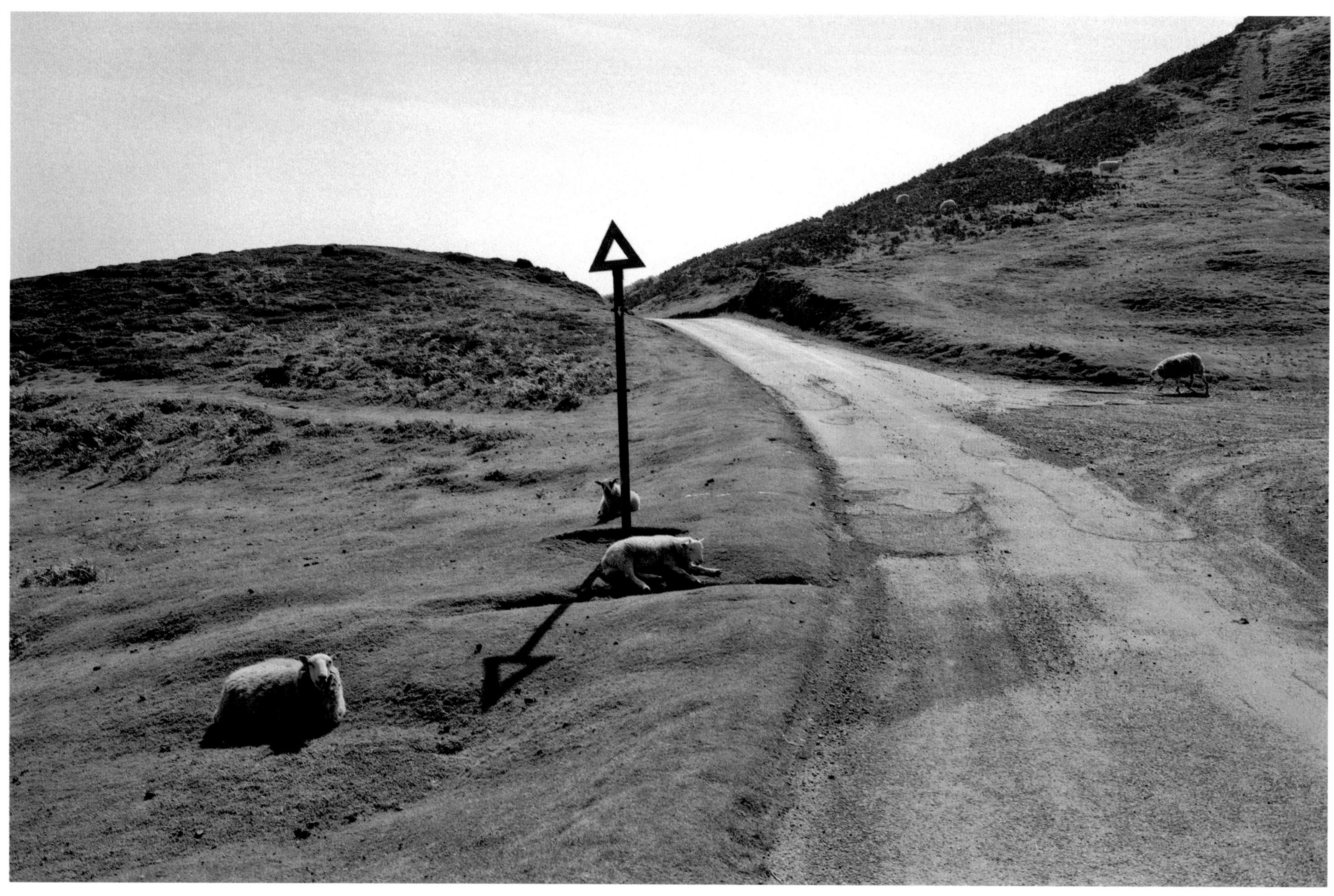

     Long Mynd, 1987

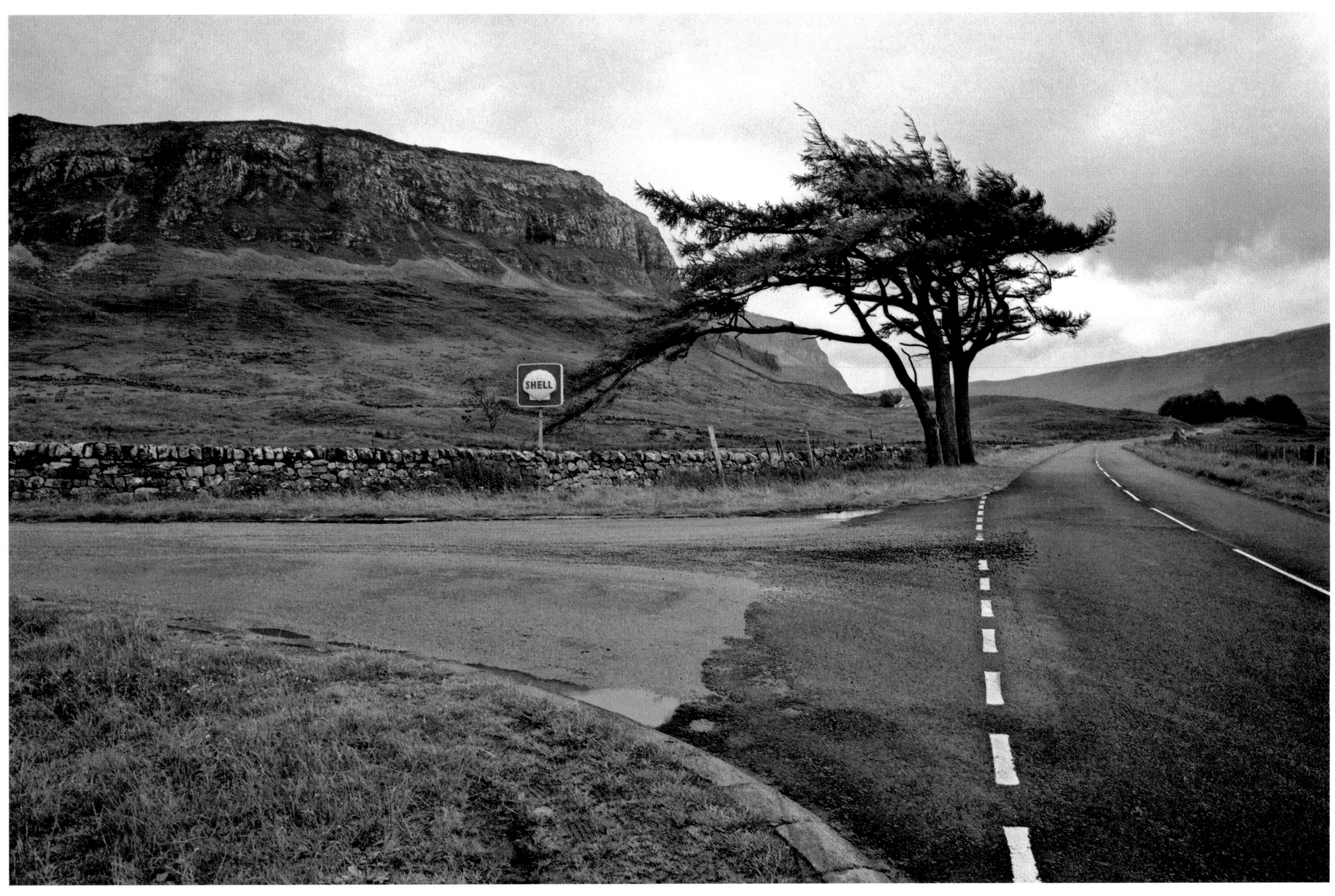

Scotland, 1984   103

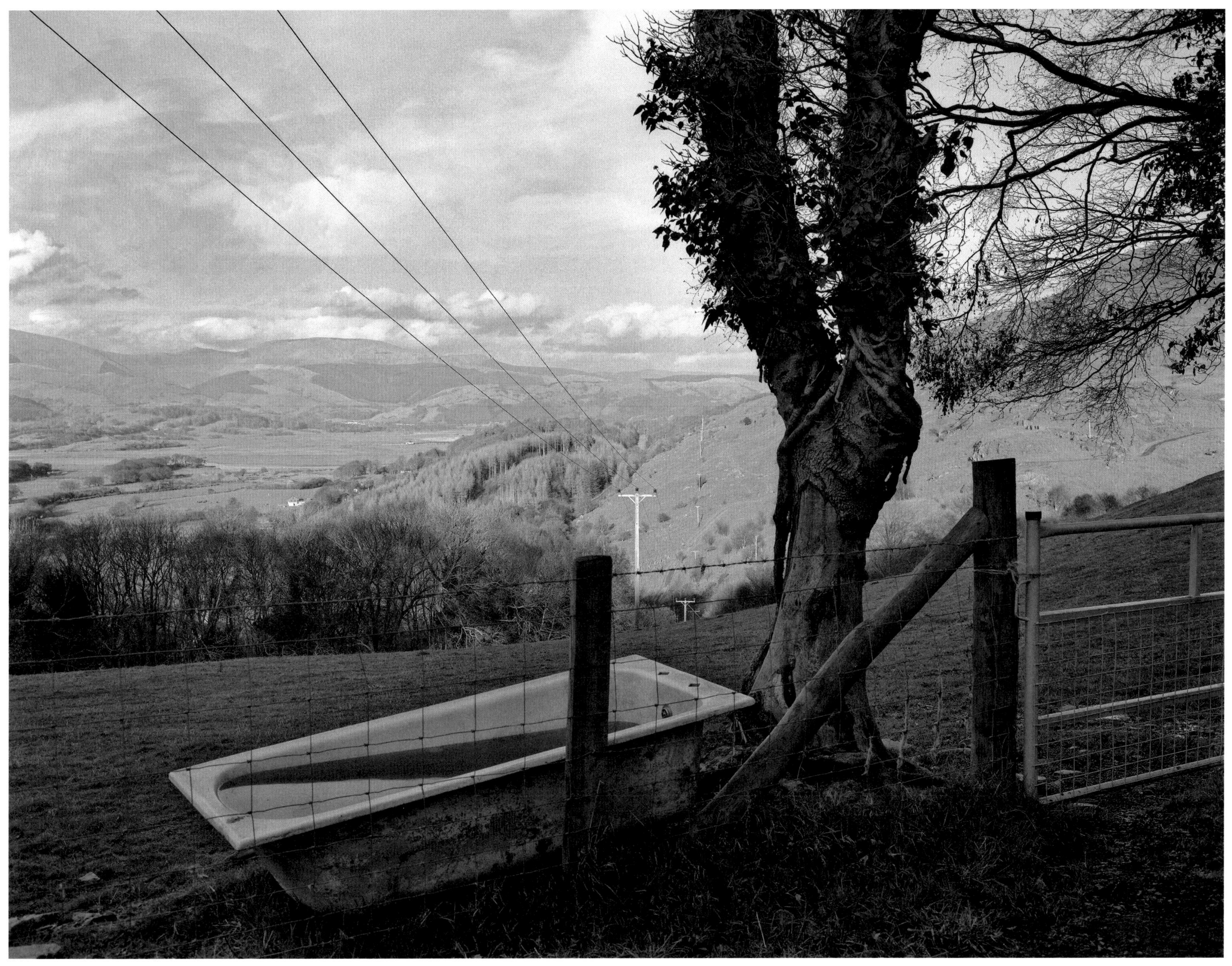

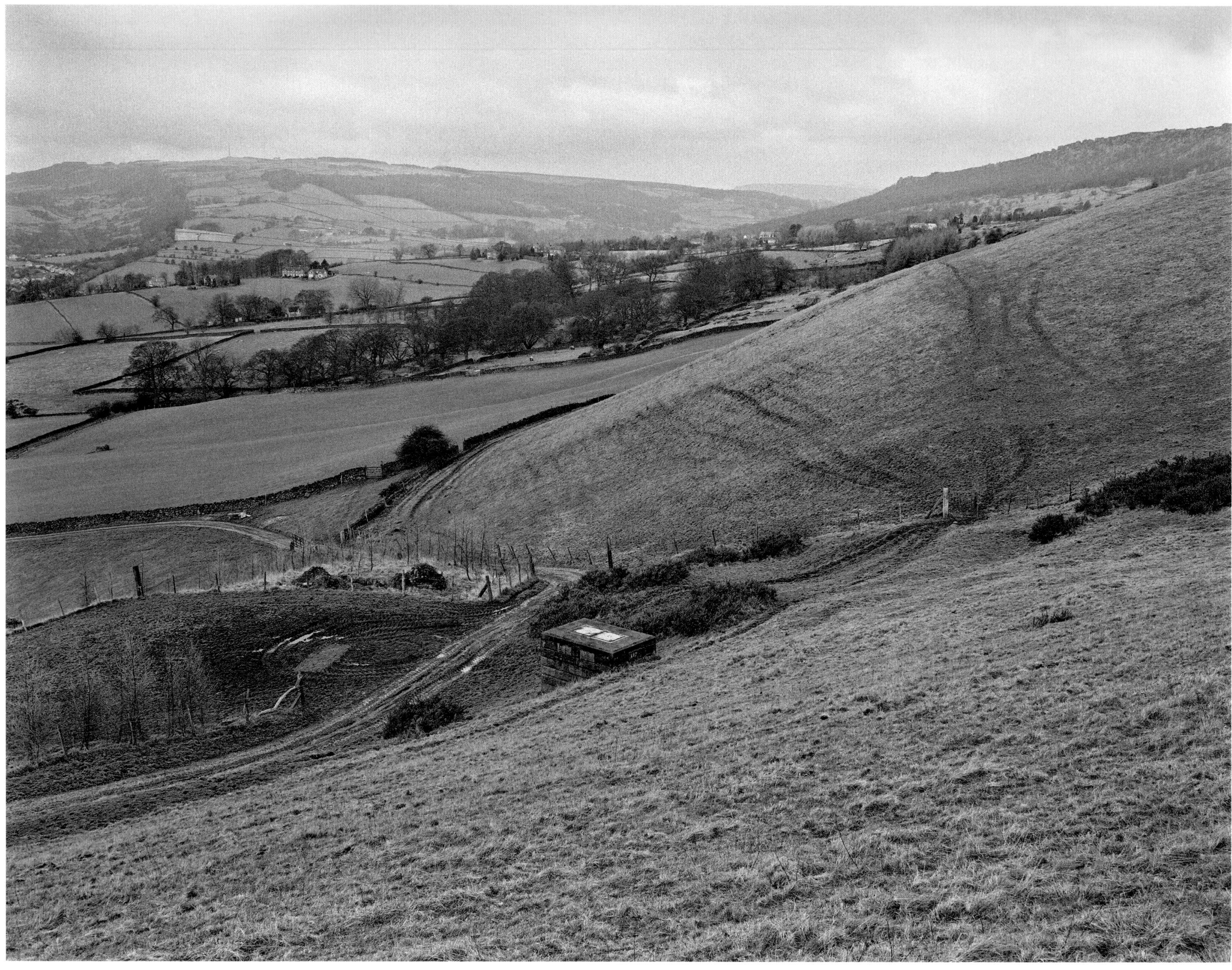

    Derbyshire, 1992

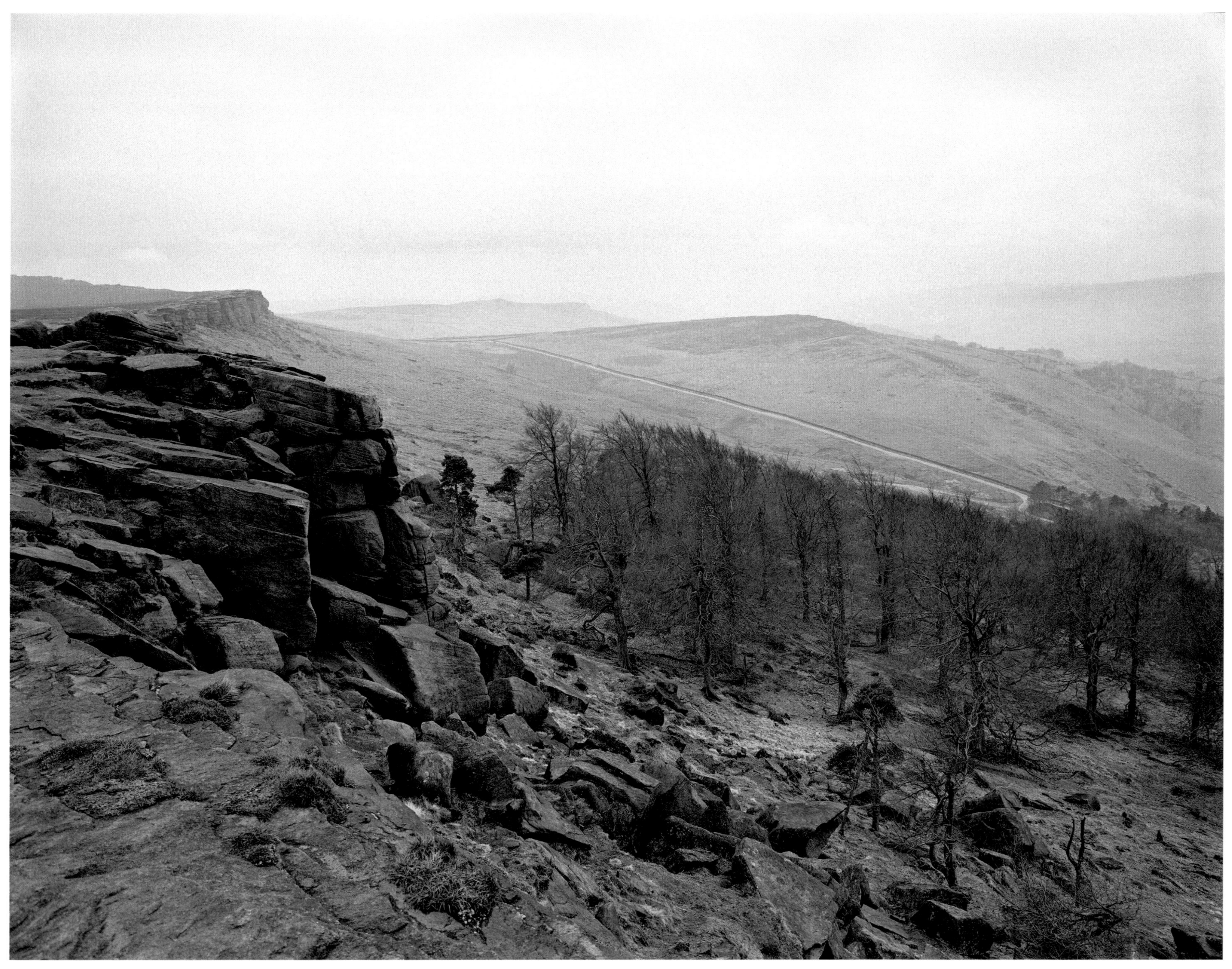

Stanage Edge, 1990

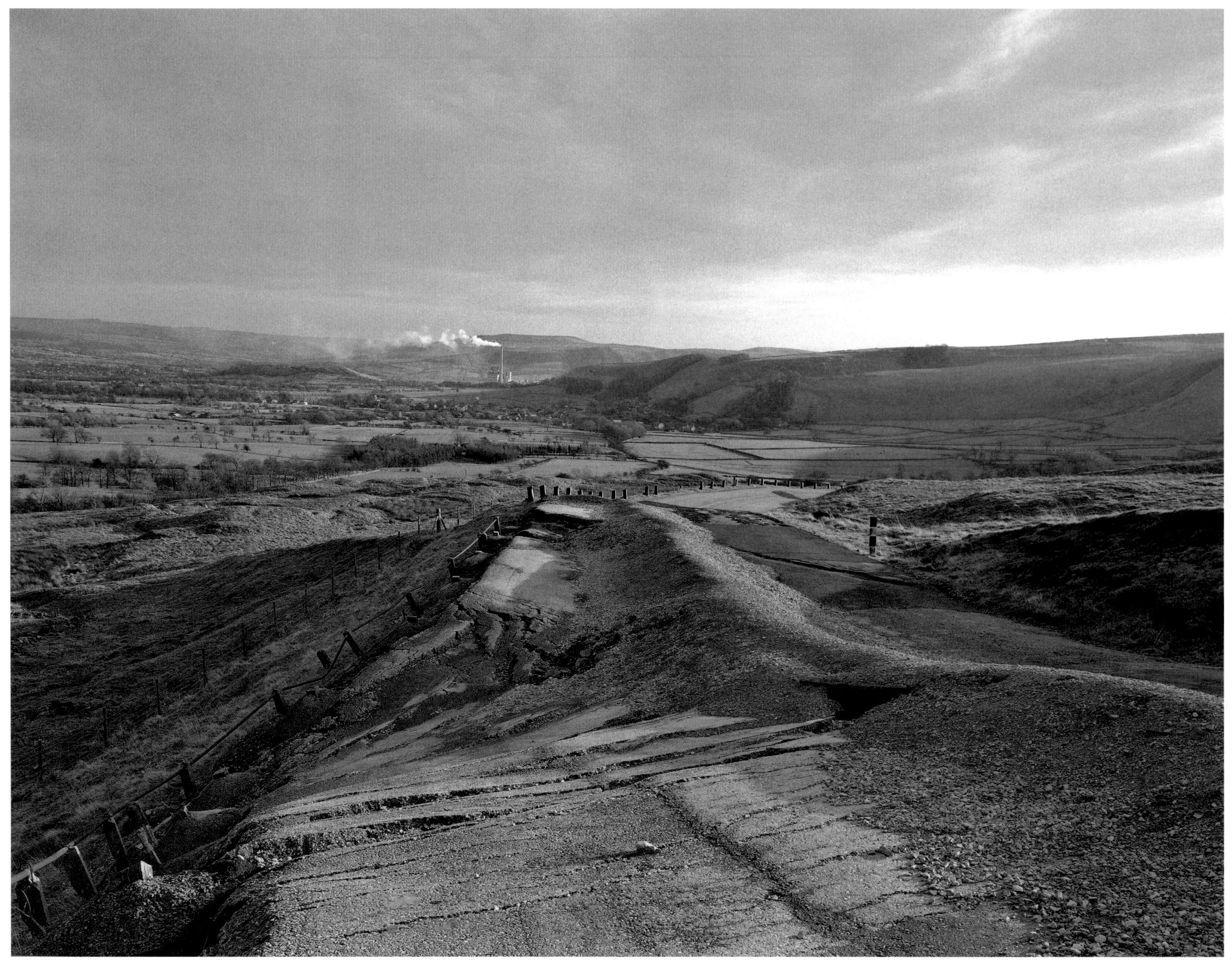

108   A625, Mam Tor, 1988

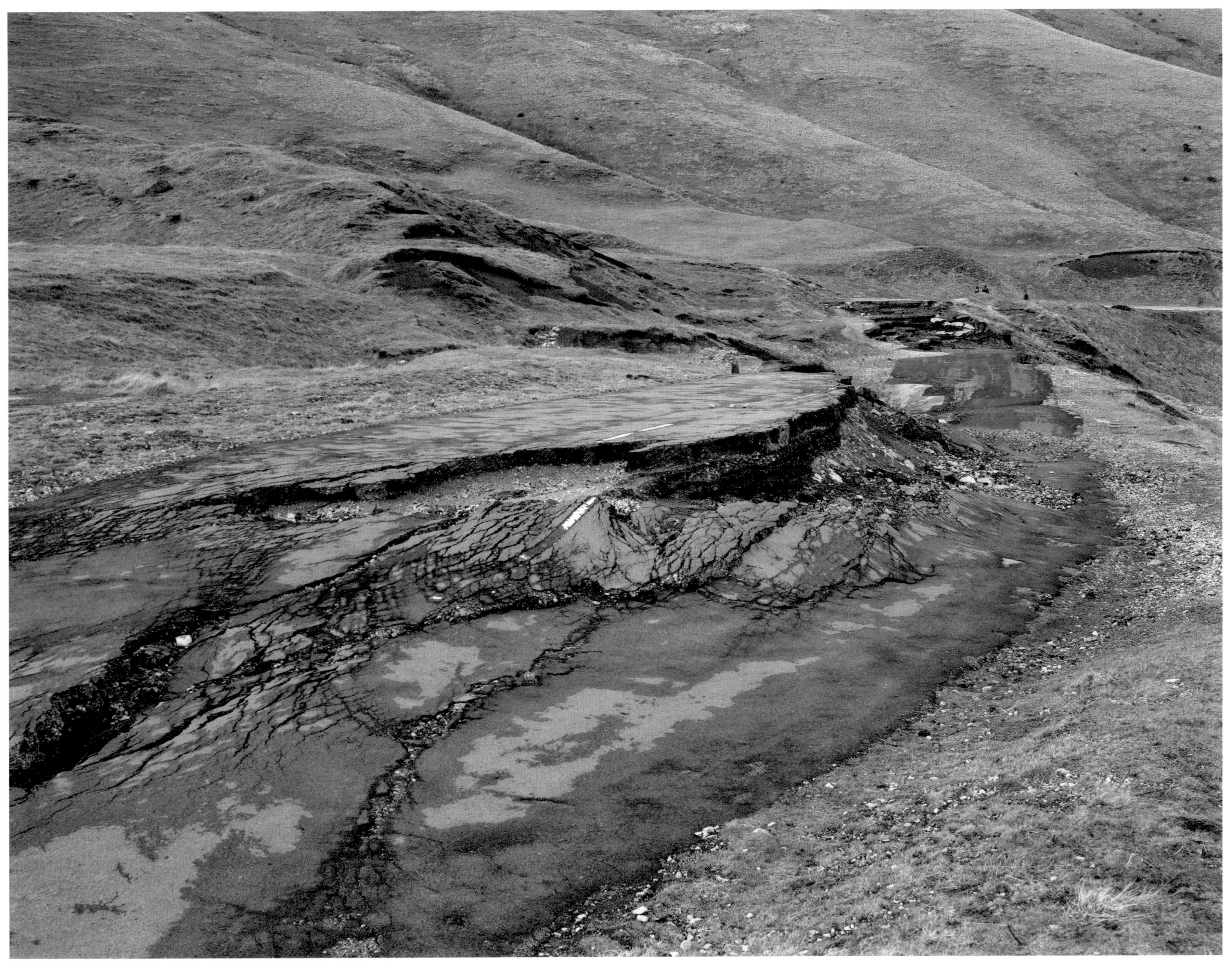

A625, Mam Tor, 1988

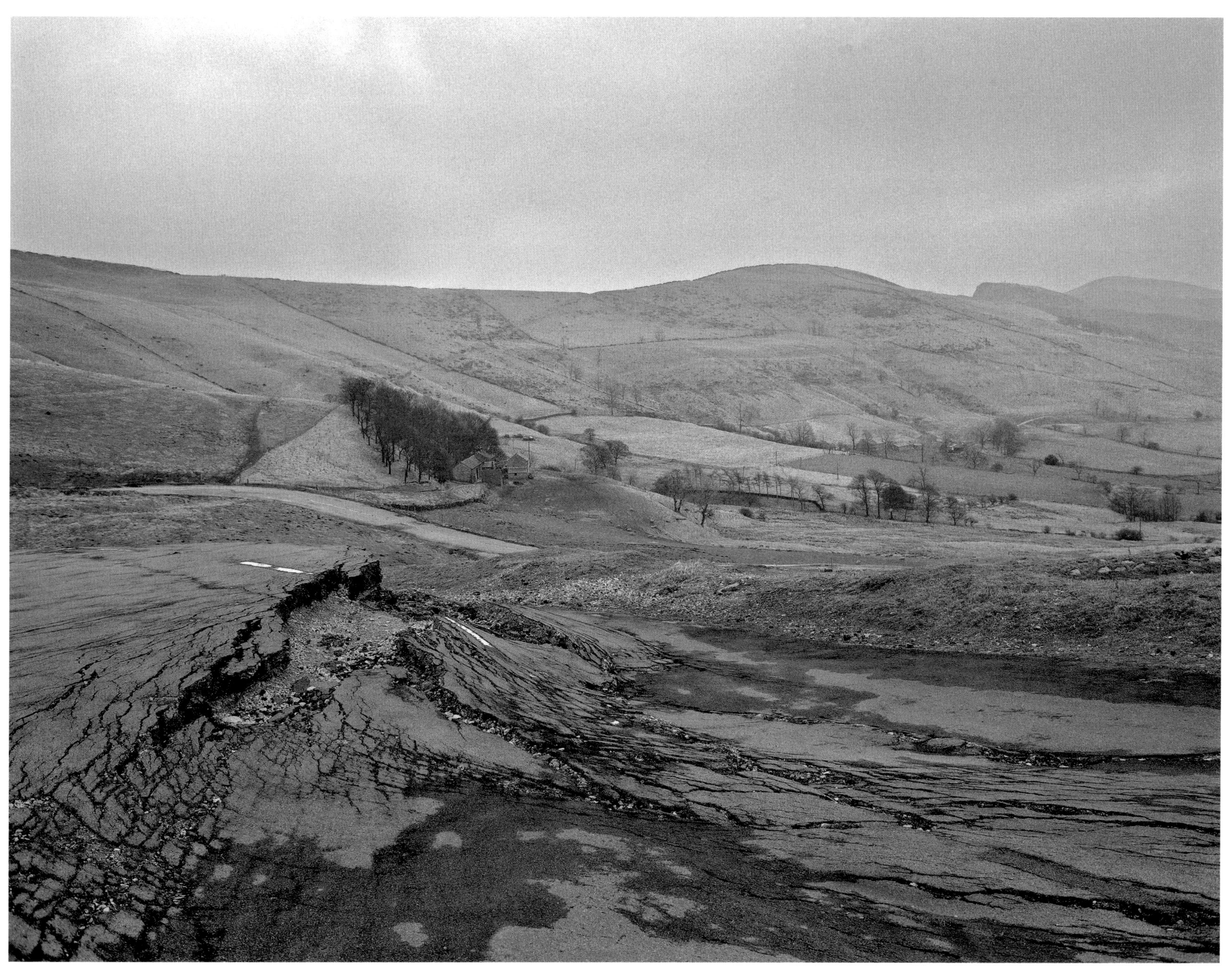

A625, Mam Tor, 1988

In memory of Jessica, Adrian and Geoff

First published in the UK in 2025 by

Dewi Lewis Publishing
8, Broomfield Road
Heaton Moor
Stockport SK4 4ND
England

www.dewilewis.com

© 2025
For the photographs: Berris Conolly
For the text: Travis Elborough
For this edition: Dewi Lewis Publishing

ISBN: 978-1-916915-19-0

Design and Edit: Dewi Lewis
Print: EBS, Verona, Italy